HONG KONG
AND
CHINA

For Better or For Worse

by Frank Ching

**Published by the China Council
of The Asia Society
and the Foreign Policy Association
New York City**

FRANK CHING is a Hong Kong-born journalist who has specialized in the coverage of China for almost two decades, first with *The New York Times* and then with *The Wall Street Journal*. He received his education at Fordham University, New York University and Columbia University and is the editor of *The New York Times Report from Red China*.

In 1979, in the wake of the establishment of diplomatic relations between the United States and the People's Republic of China, he was named Beijing correspondent of *The Wall Street Journal* and became one of the first four American newspaper reporters to be based in China since 1949.

Mr. Ching served in Beijing for four years, from 1979 to 1983, and is now writing a book on China which is to be published by William Morrow & Co.

China Council of The Asia Society

The China Council of The Asia Society is a nonpartisan, not-for-profit organization dedicated to providing public education on Chinese civilization in all of its contemporary manifestations, and on Sino-American relations. It offers a wide range of services, including publications, assistance to the news media, lectures and other public programs, and conferences. HONG KONG AND CHINA: FOR BETTER OR FOR WORSE is based in part on a conference on the future of Hong Kong held under the auspices of the China Council in New York on October 23–24, 1984.

Foreign Policy Association

The Foreign Policy Association is a private, not-for-profit, nonpartisan educational organization. Its purpose is to stimulate wider interest and more effective participation in, and greater understanding of, world affairs among American citizens. The author is responsible for factual accuracy and for the views expressed. FPA itself takes no stand on issues of U.S. foreign policy.

Cover design by Hersch Wartik; photo courtesy of Hong Kong Government. Characters at the beginning of each chapter translate as "fragrant harbor," the Chinese name for Hong Kong.

CONTENTS

Composed and printed at Science Press, Ephrata, PA
Copyright 1985 by Foreign Policy Association, Inc.
205 Lexington Avenue, New York, NY 10016
Printed in the United States of America
Library of Congress Catalog Card Number: 85-80364

香港

INTRODUCTION

On July 1, 1997, sovereignty over the territory of Hong Kong will revert from the United Kingdom to the People's Republic of China. If all has gone well between now and then, that date will mark the end of an era, but very little will actually change. The Union Jack will come down, the Chinese flag will be raised; Hong Kong, it is hoped, will continue to be a vibrant capitalist enclave, a center of manufacturing and international banking, the most important port in south China, and a magnet for tourists seeking bargain prices on everything. Hong Kong will thenceforth be a Special Administrative Region of China, the embodiment of a political arrangement unique in modern history: "one country, two systems."

Three years ago, the future of Hong Kong looked grim. With the lease on the New Territories due to expire in 1997, by mid-1982 the legal status of new 15-year mortgages and land leases was in doubt. Britain insisted on the legality of Hong Kong's colonial status under treaties dating back to 1842; the Chinese replied that the issue of sovereignty was nonnegotiable. China would eventually take back Hong Kong, with or without Britain's approval. Land values and stock prices plunged; the Hong Kong dollar lost 70 percent of its value. Key individuals and companies began making plans to seek their fortunes elsewhere.

After two years of hard and sometimes frustrating negotiations, in September 1984 both sides issued a Joint Declaration on the Hong Kong question, spelling out the territory's future in considerable detail.

For 50 years after 1997, Hong Kong, under Chinese sovereignty, will retain its present social, economic, and legal system largely intact. China, Britain, the people of Hong Kong, and interested parties around the world all now pin their hopes on the Joint Declaration. With the formal approval of that document by both sides, confidence has been restored; Hong Kong once again looks to the future with hope.

The Joint Declaration represents, in effect, a formal document of betrothal for a marriage to be consummated 12 years hence. Will the agreement stick? What is at stake? What would be the consequences of failure? HONG KONG AND CHINA: FOR BETTER OR FOR WORSE is the first book-length study in English of one of the key international agreements of the late 20th century. In it, Frank Ching details the negotiating process itself, and the agreement that emerged from it, exploring such key issues as nationality and consular relations, international aviation, the independence of Hong Kong's judicial system under a Basic Law to be drafted by the Chinese government, and the stationing of Chinese troops in the territory. The opportunities and pitfalls facing the Joint Liaison Group—charged with effecting a smooth transition of power—are explored, as are the efforts by both sides to ensure domestic and international confidence that the agreement will be adhered to. Those efforts include the historic transition, already under way, from colonial administration to representative government in Hong Kong itself.

The future of Hong Kong is itself a momentous issue, but even more is implicated in the agreement. China openly hopes to use the success of the Hong Kong Special Administrative Region under the "one country, two systems" plan as a lure for the repatriation of Taiwan. Britain has made a heavy investment of national prestige in an agreement that it has almost no means of trying to enforce.

Marriage is "for better or for worse," but many observers in Britain, China, Hong Kong, and elsewhere feel that in this case, "for better" is the only conceivable outcome: "for worse" would be intolerable. This book offers a comprehensive guide to the difficult process, already begun, of turning that imperative into concrete reality.

John S. Major, Director
China Council
of The Asia Society
June 1985

香港

1
The Negotiations

In May 1984 lines of worried customers clutching coupons stood in line outside the 47 outlets of a Hong Kong institution anxiously awaiting their turn. They had heard rumors that the company was financially unsound and did not want to suffer any losses if it went under.

It had all the earmarks of a run on a bank, but it wasn't. It was a "cake run," and the victim of the rumors was a well-known chain of cake shops known as Maria's. The panic-stricken holders of cake coupons eventually cleaned out the stores, even though Maria's staff worked overtime, with a fleet of trucks shuttling between bakeries and shops.

It was an incredible phenomenon, probably the first cake run in the world's history. Chinese brides traditionally make gifts of cake to wedding guests. In Hong Kong, the custom has evolved to the point where the bride merely gives out cake coupons, redeemable at major cake shops.

Some people, in fact, don't even bother to claim the cakes and, the more weddings they attend, the more coupons they accumulate. But then came the rumors. All of a sudden they wanted to take home the cakes due them even though they couldn't possibly eat them all before they went stale. They were in the grip of panic.

The phenomenon reflected the tensions and anxieties of a community that had been under great strain since September 1982, when Britain and the People's Republic of China (PRC) agreed to enter into negotiations that would decide the fate of the 5.5 million people of Hong Kong. The talks were held in secret, without the participation of any Hong Kong representatives.

Only a decade earlier, Hong Kong was the envy of Asia. Land prices were soaring, the standard of living was improving markedly, and the stock market was booming. Although some thoughtful people referred to Hong Kong as being "a borrowed place living on borrowed time," most of the residents were oblivious to the time bomb that had been planted in their midst before they were born.

A 19th-century lease, under which Britain took over 90 percent of the colony's territory for 99 years from a decadent and enfeebled Ching dynasty, was due to expire in 1997. A senior government official, asked about the implications of the deadline, responded: "1997? That's a very un-Hong Kong question to ask. No one here worries about it."

By the late 1970s, however, the question became more pressing. Britain had wrested Hong Kong Island and the Kowloon Peninsula from China at gunpoint (legitimized by the Treaty of Nanking of 1842 and the Convention of Peking in 1860, which ceded those areas to Britain "in perpetuity"), but the New Territories (365 square miles, consisting of a mainland area adjoining Kowloon and 235 adjacent islands) were "leased" from China rent-free in 1898 for 99 years. The leased land and the ceded areas were divided by a road now known as Boundary Street. Without the leased areas, Hong Kong would have virtually no agriculture or industry. It would lose its containerport at Kwai Chung and thus its shipping industry, the third largest in the world, and it would probably lose its airport. While the runway is south of Boundary Street, incoming and outgoing aircraft have to overfly Chinese territory to the north. Without the New Territories, the rest of Hong Kong would not be viable.

Hong Kong businessmen and foreign investors began to voice concern over the future. The colony was Asia's most important financial center and the world's third largest, after New York and London. It was also a major manufacturer, being a leading exporter of garments, electronic products, plastic goods, toys and watches. Hong Kong also had the world's largest concentration of Rolls-Royces, consumed more cognac per capita than the French, and real-estate prices were higher than those in Manhattan. Over this booming economy hung the threat of a takeover by the Communists when the lease expired. Discussions of major construction projects, such as a new airport or a second cross-harbor tunnel, were suspended. Bankers and lawyers pondered the jurisdiction of the Hong Kong government and its ability to assume responsibility for post-1997 obligations. The

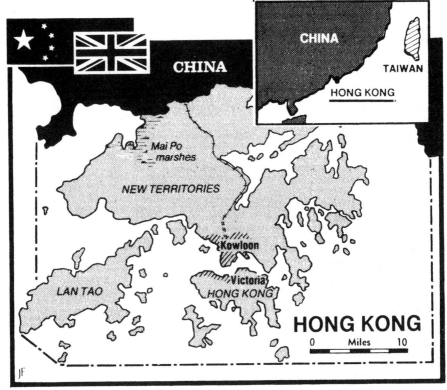

Forbes in *The Christian Science Monitor* © 1983 TCSPS.

question of land leases in the New Territories was especially acute, since all of them were due to expire on June 27, 1997, three days before the expiration of Britain's lease.

By the late 1970s, the Hong Kong government and the business community were giving serious thought to the issue. Accordingly, when Sir Murray MacLehose, governor of Hong Kong, was invited to Beijing, China's capital, in 1979, he raised the question with Chinese officials. Sir Murray returned to Hong Kong with a message from Deng Xiaoping, China's preeminent leader: "Investors should set their hearts at ease."

Uncertain future

What else transpired during that meeting with Mr. Deng has never been officially disclosed. But, according to at least one other person present, Mr. Deng made it clear that China did not recognize the three treaties and considered Hong Kong part of its territory. He said that China would certainly take back Hong Kong one day, "possibly before 1997, possibly in 1997, and possibly after 1997." It was obvious that China had not yet made up its mind about when Hong Kong should "return to the embrace of the motherland." China had too much else on its mind. More than a quarter century of mindless pursuit of ideological goals under Mao Zedong, including ten years of Cultural Revolution (a time of terror for anyone accused of "capitalist behavior"), had created monumental problems. China was busy purging the Communist party of diehard Maoists, experimenting with the greater use of market forces at the expense of the planned economy, streamlining the bureaucracy, expanding ties with foreign countries and dramatically increasing its role as a trading nation. Chinese leaders were happy to keep the Hong Kong issue on the back burner.

But Hong Kong, and Britain, kept pressing. They wanted the uncertainty of what lay beyond 1997 removed. The Hong Kong economy, they argued, would stagnate if long-term projects continued to be held in abeyance. Practical problems, such as mortgages on New Territories property, needed to be urgently resolved.

On July 1, 1982, with the New Territories lease scheduled to expire in exactly 15 years, a number of banks announced a decision to extend loan repayment terms on mortgages of property in the New Territories beyond July 1, 1997. Of course, the banks' risk was small, but it would become larger as 1997 approached. The move provided a temporary psychological boost for Hong Kong, but by then there was general feeling that Beijing must be pressed to make its intentions clear.

Meanwhile, China's leaders found themselves confronted with an unpleasant decision. The official position had always been that the three 19th-century treaties regarding Hong Kong were "unequal treaties" forced on China by imperial Britain, and hence null and void. Over and over, China had said that Hong Kong was Chinese territory, and that it would be recovered "when the time was ripe." In 1972, shortly after the PRC joined the United Nations, Ambassador Huang Hua wrote to the United Nations special committee on decolonization formally requesting that Hong Kong and Portuguese-administered Macao be removed from the list of "colonies." He wrote: "They are Chinese territories which have been under the occupation of the British and Portuguese authorities respectively. The solution to this question falls entirely within the sphere of Chinese sovereignty and does not belong to the category which is usually called 'colony.' "

Given China's oft-stated position that the three treaties were null and void, some people felt that 1997 should have no special relevance for China and that the Chinese authorities might be persuaded not to oppose continuation of British administration in Hong Kong beyond 1997. As the British government continued to press for an answer, Beijing's aging leaders, who had a profound sense of history as well as a deep concern as to how they would be depicted by later generations of Chinese, decided that they had to take back Hong Kong. That decision was made by the spring of 1982. Starting in May, the Chinese deliberately began to leak details of their decision to the left-wing press and to unofficial Hong Kong delegations visiting Beijing.

Thatcher visit: The 'first phase' of negotiations

Mrs. Margaret Thatcher, the British prime minister, visited Beijing in September 1982 and raised the subject of Hong Kong with both Premier Zhao Ziyang and Mr. Deng. Both events were carefully stage-managed by the Chinese. Just before Premier Zhao's scheduled meeting with Mrs. Thatcher, he casually wandered into a group of Hong Kong reporters and disclosed the Chinese position. "There is no need for people in Hong Kong to worry about the future," he said. "Of course China will recover sovereignty over Hong Kong. But I think the question of sovereignty will not influence Hong Kong's prosperity and stability." By saying in public what he would later tell Mrs. Thatcher in private, he made it clear that China's position was unalterable. This is a diplomatic ploy often favored by Chinese officials.

Mrs. Thatcher's visit to Beijing was marked by an incident that appeared portentous to Hong Kong reporters. Descending the steps of the Great Hall of the People in Tiananmen Square after the two and a half hour meeting with Premier Zhao, she slipped and fell on her hands and knees, making what appeared to be a crude kowtow in the direction of Mao's mausoleum.

The next day Mrs. Thatcher met Mr. Deng. The meeting was cloaked in secrecy but, according to well-placed sources, Mr. Deng did not mince his words, telling Mrs. Thatcher that the question of China's sovereignty over Hong Kong was not negotiable. When China recovers sovereignty, he said, the British flag and the British governor would have to go, and China would take steps to ensure the territory's prosperity.

Mrs. Thatcher emphasized the importance of continuing Hong Kong's links with Britain if the territory was to be preserved as a bustling commercial and financial center but left open the possibility that something could be worked out to satisfy China's demand that Britain recognize Beijing's sovereignty over Hong Kong. Mr. Deng then responded that, if he were to extend the lease, he would go down in history as another Li Hung-chang, the Ching dynasty diplomat who signed the 1898 Convention of Peking, and whose name is now synonymous with national betrayal. (The unfortunate Mr. Li was befriended by General Ulysses S. Grant when he was in China during his world tour. Two trees, a gift from China sent by Mr. Li, stand today behind Grant's tomb in New York City.)

The British and Chinese leaders talked for two hours and twenty minutes. At the end of their meeting a joint communiqué was issued: "Today the leaders of both countries held far-reaching talks in a friendly atmosphere on the future of Hong Kong. Both leaders made clear their respective positions on this subject. They agreed to enter talks through diplomatic channels following the visit, with the common aim of maintaining the stability and prosperity of Hong Kong."

That last sentence marked the only point of agreement between the two countries. It also marked the beginning of what would turn out to be a two-year-long nightmare for Hong Kong, when its fate was being decided by Britain and China in secret diplomatic negotiations, marked at times by mutual recriminations so violent that the talks were in danger of collapsing.

The distance between the two sides was immediately apparent. At the press conference held by Mrs. Thatcher in Beijing after her meeting with Mr. Deng, she was infuriated to learn from a reporter that the official Chinese news agency, Xinhua, had appended to the joint statement a unilateral Chinese declaration: "The Chinese government's position on the recovery of the whole region of Hong Kong is unequivocal and known to all." The Chinese statement laid bare the differences between the two sides that the diplomatically worded joint communiqué was meant to hide. During her press conference, Mrs. Thatcher not only asserted the validity of the three 19th-century treaties, but said that a country that does not honor one treaty cannot be trusted to abide by other treaties. "We stick to our treaties," she declared pugnaciously.

Six days after Mrs. Thatcher's departure from Beijing, at a reception to mark China's National Day, this author remarked to a Chinese official that perhaps the Hong Kong problem could be resolved by Britain forgoing its political claims of sovereignty over Hong Kong in return for Chinese consent to the continuation of British administration. "That's the British position," the official declared. "How can there be a British governor after China regains its sovereignty?" This was the question at the heart of the dispute.

Economic jitters

In Hong Kong, Mrs. Thatcher was roundly applauded for having taken a tough stance. At a press conference, she again declared that the three treaties were "valid under international law." They can be varied, she said, but not unilaterally abrogated. She apparently meant that they could be replaced by a new agreement. She insisted that Britain had not yielded sovereignty over Hong Kong. A local newspaper carried a banner headline the following morning: "Confidence Restored!" Succeeding days, however, made it clear that her tough talk, far from reassuring people, had convinced many that difficult times lay ahead. Both the stock market and the Hong Kong dollar plummeted. In a six-day trading period, the Hang Seng Index fell 280 points, wiping out over 25 percent of the value of the shares. And the Hong Kong dollar, which in the early 1970s was one of the world's strongest currencies, started its long downward slide.

Meanwhile, the real-estate boom had run its course. Supply outstripped demand and property prices started to drop. The political uncertainty helped to keep the property market in the doldrums for the next two years.

Mrs. Thatcher's inauspicious visit to Beijing heralded the beginning of what later came to be known euphemistically as the "first phase" of negotiations, which lasted for nine months. No information was disclosed by either the Chinese or the British during this period, as Prime Minister Thatcher had insisted on confidentiality for the talks.

Not only were people in Hong Kong kept in the dark; the British even refused to brief their closest allies. Efforts by American diplomats in Beijing, Hong Kong, London, and Washington to obtain information proved fruitless. The British were holding their cards close to their chest.

China's precondition: British renunciation of sovereignty

Actually, this nine-month period, from September 1982 to June 1983, was characterized by total deadlock. The Chinese insisted that the British acknowledge Chinese sovereignty over Hong Kong. The British responded that, in the joint communiqué, there had been no reference to any preconditions to the start of negotiations. The Chinese insisted that their demands were nonnegotiable; Britain, on the other hand, felt that if it conceded sovereignty right at the start, it would have very little left with which to bargain. The British tried to draw the Chinese out on what they had in mind for Hong Kong, hinting first obliquely and later broadly that some kind of British concession on sovereignty was possible, but the Chinese refused to talk about substantive issues unless the British first acknowledged Chinese sovereignty. The Chinese, too, dropped hints, saying that if Britain would only take this one step, a satisfactory solution could be reached on all other problems and Britain's economic interests in Hong Kong would be protected.

At this time, the Chinese resorted to Mao's old strategy of isolating the primary antagonist by uniting with as many other people as possible. Beijing began an elaborate campaign to court the people of Hong Kong, receiving delegations of all types and explaining to them its policies for the territory. In February 1983, it appointed 140 Hong Kong and Macao residents to the National People's Congress and the Chinese People's Political Consultative Conference, a united-front organization on which the Communist party calls for advice but which has no real power.

Even before the Thatcher visit, China had in effect been out-flanking the British by inviting delegations from Hong Kong to the Chinese capital and telling them, ostensibly in confidence, China's plans for Hong Kong.

The Chinese sought to reassure Hong Kong that, even though the British would have to go, nothing much would change for a long time, which was initially defined as 15 years. Hong Kong, it was said, would be treated as a special region of China, and would be run by Hong Kong people themselves. Visitors from Hong Kong were told that such bourgeois pastimes as dancing and horse racing could continue even after China takes back Hong Kong in 1997, although the "Royal" will have to come out of the name "Royal Hong Kong Jockey Club."

In the absence of hard information about the negotiations, specula-tion was rife. In January 1983, the British concept that any agreement on Hong Kong had to be acceptable to Britain, China and Hong Kong was vigorously condemned by China's propaganda machinery as a "three-legged stool" theory. According to China, this approach gave Hong Kong a status equal to that of China and Britain, and it rejected it out of hand as an infringement on Chinese sovereignty.

In May 1983, with the two sides still deadlocked, a 12-person delegation from Hong Kong, dubbed the Young Professionals by the Chinese, arrived in Beijing. Its leader was Allen Lee, a businessman who is also an appointed member of the Legislative Council. The council, Hong Kong's legislature, consists of senior civil servants and appointed members of the public. The group tried to convince Chinese officials that there was a confidence crisis in Hong Kong, and that China's plan for Hong Kong people to run Hong Kong as a capitalist enclave in socialist China would not work. What the group and probably the vast majority of the Hong Kong people wanted was maintenance of the status quo, with the British acting as a buffer between a politically volatile China and a stable, prosperous Hong Kong. However, the delegation, which was considered "pro-British" by the Chinese, was unable to get Beijing to change its policy. Meanwhile, the Hong Kong dollar had sunk to a record low, closing at 7.10 to the U.S. dollar on May 28, 1983.

British concession

The deadlock was finally broken through the personal intervention of Mrs. Thatcher. The prime minister sent two private messages to Premier Zhao. Neither the content nor the fact the two messages were sent has been disclosed until now. Mrs. Thatcher proposed that substantive negotiations could begin, with the understanding that Britain was fully aware of China's position on sovereignty. The Chinese were informed that, if a solution could be found whereby

Hong Kong's stability and prosperity would be maintained, the prime minister "would be prepared to recommend it to the British Parliament," and sovereignty would be conceded at that point. Britain in effect was suggesting that the sovereignty issue was not really a problem, but first there had to be discussion in considerable detail of the two governments' respective ideas on the future of Hong Kong. The Chinese accepted this proposal.

Accordingly, on July 1, 1983, Beijing and London jointly announced that the "second-phase" talks—the first formal talks—would begin on July 12. From that time until the draft agreement was initialed more than 14 months later, 22 rounds of talks were held, with each round lasting two days.

The absent party: Hong Kong

Both Britain and China claimed to speak for Hong Kong, Britain as the actual administrator of the territory for the last 140 years and China as the champion of its "Hong Kong compatriots" who had been under the colonial yoke for so long, and who were finally to be reunited with the motherland. The result was that Hong Kong had no direct voice in determining its own fate.

Britain promised to strive for an agreement that would be acceptable to the people of Hong Kong. It attempted to ascertain their wishes by using the opinion-gathering machinery in Hong Kong—from the District Boards, which assist in running each of the territory's 18 districts, at the bottom of the scale, to the Executive Council, which appoints advisers to the governor, at the top. Though the talks were secret, the Executive Councillors were privy to information about them. As the governor's advisers, they also served as a conduit to apprise him of the wishes of the general public.

On the Chinese side, Xinhua, left-wing newspapers and other Chinese institutions such as the Bank of China were able to keep Beijing informed on the mood in Hong Kong. Moreover, a stream of delegations headed north from Hong Kong to voice their views to Chinese officials. In this way, both sides undoubtedly had a fairly good general idea of the wishes of the Hong Kong people.

Round one

The first round of talks, held July 12–13, 1983, ended with a simple joint communiqué reporting that the session was "useful and constructive." The second round of talks, also held in July, ended with an announcement by the two sides that it had been "useful." After the third round in August, the two sides issued a statement merely saying that talks had been "held." Things were clearly not going well.

In Hong Kong, the optimism of July gave way to anxiety. On

August 15, Hu Yaobang, the Communist party leader, told Japanese journalists that China would take back Hong Kong on July 1, 1997. It was the first time a Chinese official had publicly pinpointed a date. Mr. Hu said that China had developed "a complete set of policies" for running Hong Kong. He asserted that China respected history and so intended to recover Hong Kong in 1997, no sooner and no later.

Mr. Hu's statement to the Japanese was part of China's psychological war against the British. While diplomats were thrusting and parrying at the negotiating table, the Chinese were waging a war of words on the side.

During August, left-wing unions in Hong Kong entered the picture. The unions, including the Motor Transport Workers Union and the Hong Kong Union of Chinese Workers in Western Style Employment, declared that China's plan for the recovery of sovereignty over Hong Kong "is completely in line with the wish of Hong Kong's numerous labor compatriots." Their stand was immediately praised by the pro-Communist press. *Ta Kung Pao,* one of the main left-wing newspapers, said in an editorial: "Theirs [the left-wing unions'] is the true public opinion."

Public opinion was a major issue in the Sino-British negotiations. *Ta Kung Pao* made this plain when it attacked Prime Minister Thatcher, saying she was the first to start playing the "public opinion card." The paper concluded: "More than 90 percent of the population here are of Chinese stock and they will realize the change of situation. Whatever more magic the Hong Kong government tries to play with the 'public opinion card,' the majority of the Hong Kong people will realize their tricks. . . ."

Although the official records of the talks are still wrapped in secrecy, and will remain so for at least 30 years, it is possible to reconstruct what happened in those early rounds by piecing together what appeared in the press and by talking to sources in a position to know, including people who played a direct part in the negotiations. During the first three rounds of negotiations, the British undertook to explain to the Chinese the factors that accounted for Hong Kong's success. They attributed Hong Kong's prosperity in large part to its ability to participate, through its British links, in international trading arrangements, such as the General Agreement on Tariffs and Trade (GATT) and the Multifiber Arrangement. They explained the virtues of the British legal system and the rights and freedoms guaranteed under the rule of law, as well as the orderly administration of Hong Kong provided by the British government, which had the support and confidence of the public.

As the exposition went on, the Chinese became more and more angry. From their standpoint, the British were really building a case for being indispensable. Chinese anger spilled over into Hong Kong.

When the British negotiators bluntly told their Chinese counterparts that Hong Kong people had no confidence in the Chinese Communists, Beijing instructed left-wing labor unions in Hong Kong to state publicly their ardent desire to be reunited with the motherland. When the British diplomats asserted that Hong Kong's prosperity was due to the colony's link with Britain, a spate of articles appeared in the left-wing press arguing that Hong Kong's prosperity was the result of the hard-working Chinese in the territory, with the support of the motherland, which provided food and water at low prices.

The people of Hong Kong were caught in a vise. The more pressure Britain put on China, or China on Britain, the more they felt squeezed. Those who possessed capital or professional skills sent their money abroad and made plans to emigrate to such countries as the United States and Canada. Passports of a wide variety of countries, including Portugal, Paraguay, the Dominican Republic, and even Tonga, were sought. Immigration lawyers descended on Hong Kong to hold seminars and offer their services. Foreign governments offered incentives to lure capital from Hong Kong. Because the Hong Kong government does not monitor the flow of money into and out of the colony, it is not possible to quantify the amount of flight capital, but it was probably considerable. Even within the territory, ordinary citizens were converting their savings from Hong Kong dollar accounts to U.S. dollar accounts as the local currency continued to fall.

The steady decline in the value of the Hong Kong dollar hurt Beijing badly, since China gets roughly a third of its annual foreign exchange from or through Hong Kong. The Chinese suspected Britain of deliberately manipulating the money markets. There is no conclusive evidence that such was the case. However, the remarks of Sir John Bremridge, Hong Kong's financial secretary, appear to have contributed to the continued fall of the local currency.

Asked if the government was taking action to support the Hong Kong dollar, he replied: "It's not possible to fix the exchange rate of the Hong Kong dollar to any particular level. This must depend upon the forces of the marketplace." This was seen as a clear signal that the government had no intention of rescuing the currency. Moreover, the financial secretary turned down suggestions that the 10 percent withholding tax on Hong Kong dollar deposits be removed. Since there was no tax on foreign currency accounts, some people switched from Hong Kong dollars to U.S. dollars. Before the fourth round of talks began in September, the Hong Kong dollar had sunk to less than eight to the U.S. dollar. Mr. Deng is reported to have said that even if the Hong Kong dollar should drop to 20 to 1 U.S. dollar, China would still not give in. Premier Zhao and other officials said, "No country can put prosperity ahead of sovereignty."

While the issue on the surface was one of sovereignty, the real battle

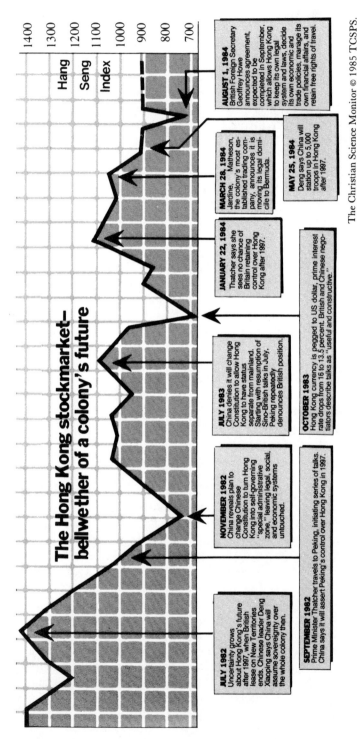

The Hong Kong stockmarket—bellwether of a colony's future

Hang Seng Index

1400
1300
1200
1100
1000
900
800
700

JULY 1982
Uncertainty grows about Hong Kong's future after 1997, when British lease on New Territories ends. Chinese leader Deng Xiaoping says China will assume sovereignty over the whole colony then.

SEPTEMBER 1982
Prime Minister Thatcher travels to Peking, initiating series of talks. China says it will assert Peking's control over Hong Kong in 1997.

NOVEMBER 1982
China reveals plan to change Chinese Constitution to turn Hong Kong into self-governing "special administrative zone," leaving legal, social, and economic systems untouched.

JULY 1983
China denies it will change Constitution to allow Hong Kong to have status separate from mainland. Starting with resumption of Sino-British talks in July, Peking repeatedly denounces British position.

OCTOBER 1983
Hong Kong currency is pegged to US dollar, prime interest rate drops from 16 to 13.5 percent. British and Chinese negotiators describe talks as "useful and constructive."

JANUARY 22, 1984
Thatcher says she sees no chance of Britain retaining control over Hong Kong after 1997.

MARCH 28, 1984
Jardine, Matheson, the colony's most established trading company, announces it is moving its legal domicile to Bermuda.

MAY 25, 1984
Deng says China will station up to 5,000 troops in Hong Kong after 1997.

AUGUST 1, 1984
British Foreign Secretary Geoffrey Howe announces agreement, expected to be completed in September, which allows Hong Kong to keep its own legal system and laws, decide its own economic and trade policies, manage its own financial affairs, and retain free rights of travel.

The Christian Science Monitor © 1985 TCSPS.

at this point was over whether the British could continue to administer Hong Kong beyond 1997. China maintained that sovereignty without administrative rights was hollow—form with no substance.

By the end of the third round, held August 2 and 3, the deadlock was total. During the seven-week summer recess the British reassessed the situation. As intensive consultations were held with members of the Executive Council in Hong Kong, the British embassy in Beijing and the Foreign Office in London, the anxiety level in Hong Kong kept rising. The decline of the Hong Kong dollar inevitably led to price increases, and this in turn created social unrest. On September 18, a rally was held in Victoria Park, attended by 3,000 people, to protest the increase in prices, especially of electricity.

Round four

In this atmosphere, the British were faced with a difficult decision: Should they continue to be adamant and take the risk of aborting the talks and precipitating a crisis in Hong Kong, or should they accept the Chinese demands and hope for the best? The British decided to give in but, before making another concession, they decided to hang tough for one more round. So, when the fourth round was held on September 22 and 23, the British stuck to their guns. So did the Chinese. That round marked the low point of the entire two-year process.

Yao Guang, the chief Chinese negotiator, obliquely accused the British of having manufactured the currency crisis to put pressure on China. The phlegmatic Chinese diplomat told his British counterpart, the dour Sir Percy Cradock, with great solemnity that the currency problem was a British problem, and one that Britain was fully capable of resolving. When news of the stalemate reached Hong Kong, the local currency plummeted to 8.83 to the American dollar, the biggest fall in its history. Some shops were starting to quote prices in U.S. dollars. The Hong Kong dollar was rapidly losing its position as a hard currency. At the same time, the Hong Kong stock market slumped, with the index dropping by 65.58 points to 785.48.

Panic in Hong Kong

On September 24, 1983, the day after the fourth round ended, the floor gave way again and the Hong Kong dollar fell to 9.50 to the U.S. dollar. Panic gripped Hong Kong. Overnight, supermarkets were cleaned out. People stocked up on everything from food to toilet paper. Business with Hong Kong's trading partners was affected, because no one was willing to have prices denominated in Hong Kong dollars anymore, given the volatility of the currency. Vegetable dealers reported that Taiwan (the Republic of China) had decided to halt all shipments to the colony because the Hong Kong dollar no longer commanded confidence. People watched in horror as their life savings shrank to a fraction of the original value. Fear spread that the Hong Kong government was impotent in the face of the greatest crisis facing the colony since World War II.

The governor, Sir Edward Youde, returned to Hong Kong from Beijing at the height of the crisis. He immediately announced that steps would be taken to save the Hong Kong dollar. Financial Secretary Sir John, in Washington for a meeting of the International Monetary Fund, rushed back to Hong Kong to devise remedial measures. That same evening, Richard Luce, the Foreign Office minister responsible for Hong Kong, arrived in the colony. "Have confidence in yourselves just as the British government have confidence in you and are committed to you," he said in an arrival statement.

If Britain deliberately manipulated the foreign currency market to put pressure on China, it failed miserably. "If we play rough with China, the blood on the rug would be Hong Kong's blood," one British official said.

The Hong Kong government took belated action to rescue the local currency. Quite astonishingly, it almost immediately halted the slide. Within a matter of days, the Hong Kong dollar had recovered to 8.37 to the U.S. dollar. And when Sir John returned to Hong Kong, he declared: "What I can say regarding the dollar is that those people selling Hong Kong dollars at this juncture are going to get their fingers badly burned." Despite his earlier claim that market forces had to determine the value of the currency, Sir John pegged the Hong Kong dollar to the greenback, at 7.80 to the U.S. dollar. He also abolished the 10 percent withholding tax on Hong Kong dollar deposits. The government's success seemed to bear out the Chinese charge, repeated in the Hong Kong media, that the currency crisis, even if it had not been created by the Hong Kong government, was well within its ability to resolve.

On September 28, the British broke the veil of restraint and castigated China's use of the media to attack Britain as "megaphone diplomacy." But the pressure on Britain continued as China reaffirmed its intention to announce unilaterally its plans for the future of Hong Kong if an agreement with Britain was not reached by September 1984.

Britain's back door

The British yielded. Prime Minister Thatcher informed Premier Zhao of Britain's conditional agreement to sever all its ties with Hong Kong after 1997 and said Britain would concede sovereignty over all of Hong Kong. This British concession marked the biggest breakthrough in the Sino-British talks. From that point on, it was almost inevitable that an agreement would eventually be reached. When the fifth round ended on October 20, the phrase "useful and constructive" reappeared. The Hong Kong public was kept in the dark. The situation was further muddled by Mrs. Thatcher. In spite of her secret message to Premier Zhao agreeing to the termination of the British administration of Hong Kong in 1997, the prime minister said on October 31, in a British Broadcasting Corporation worldwide phone-in program: "Well, these kind of things [a British presence in Hong Kong after 1997] are exactly what we're now negotiating about. And obviously we think that the British link is very, very important indeed, because it is partly responsible for the kind of success we've had in Hong Kong."

The first year of negotiations was described in a White Paper issued by the British in this way: "Following extensive discussion, however, it became clear that the continuation of British administration after 1997 would not be acceptable to China in any form." Once that was clear, the White Paper said, Britain shifted to another tack and proposed that the two sides discuss "what effective measures other than continued British administration might be devised to maintain the stability and prosperity of Hong Kong and explore further the Chinese ideas about the future. . . ."

Negotiations accelerate

From this point on, the two sides were able to work together relatively smoothly. China, having won the battles on sovereignty and administration, was willing to listen as Britain detailed the complexities of Hong Kong, its international economic and financial role, the necessity for adapting rapidly to changes in its markets, the Hong Kong legal system, and the territory's obligations under a network of treaties and international organizations that it had joined by virtue of the British umbrella. The Chinese, on their part, had to spell out details of their proposal that Hong Kong would be given a "high degree of autonomy" as a special administrative region of China that would practice not the socialist system of the mainland but capitalism. In the end, the amount of detail in the final agreement was the greatest achievement of the British negotiators. The agreement and the Basic Law enshrining its principles will, after 1997, be the only buffer between Hong Kong and its Communist masters in Beijing.

To speed up the process, the British and Chinese decided to supplement the formal sessions with informal contacts between the two delegations. The informal contacts would also provide opportunities for the two sides to elaborate on the ideas discussed at the formal sessions. In public, however, the British continued to maintain that they would not be rushed by any artificial deadline imposed by the Chinese.

China had set a deadline of September 1984 for completion of the negotiations. If there was no agreement by then, Chinese leaders said, Beijing would unilaterally announce its policies for Hong Kong after 1997. No reason was ever advanced for the selection of that particular deadline, but since Prime Minister Thatcher had visited China in September 1982, this meant the Chinese were giving the negotiations two years. It is likely that Chinese leaders, such as Mr. Deng, wanted to be able to add an agreement on Hong Kong as a feather in their cap before October 1, 1984, the 35th anniversary of the establishment of the People's Republic of China, when massive public celebrations were scheduled.

Almost as soon as the British capitulated, China ceased its public attacks. On November 16, the day after the sixth round was held, the Chinese foreign ministry spokesman told reporters at a news briefing that relations between China and Britain were normal. Chinese officials continued to make reassuring noises, directed both at the Hong Kong community and at foreign investors. Ji Pengfei, director of the Hong Kong-Macao office, said there would be no changes in Hong Kong's system or lifestyle for 50 years after 1997. Hu Yaobang, the Communist party leader, told Japanese visitors that investors did not have to worry about their assets in Hong Kong. Peng Zhen, head of the National People's Congress, assured Hong Kong residents that communism would not be imposed on the territory.

The session of December 7 and 8, the last round of 1983, reflected the changed atmosphere of the talks. The British were no longer on the defensive. Instead, they were firing off questions. To what extent will Hong Kong be autonomous? What will the Basic Law include? What laws will be used? What does it mean to say that the legal system will be "basically unchanged"? What will change? What language will be used in the courts?

The British proposed that foreign judges from British Commonwealth countries, such as Australia, New Zealand and India, be allowed to serve in Hong Kong, as well as British judges. The Chinese were reluctant. Since the judiciary is an arm of the government, they felt that allowing foreign judges to officiate in Hong Kong might be an infringement of Chinese sovereignty. (Ultimately, China accepted this British proposal.) The Chinese explained that in the future the governor and the chief officials would have to be approved by Beijing after they have been chosen by the people of Hong Kong. That round concluded with the encouraging public announcement that the two sides had reviewed "the progress made so far" in these negotiations. It was the first open acknowledgment of progress in the talks.

New round, new team

The January 1984 session was held amid expectations of a quick settlement. Both delegations were headed by new men. Sir Richard Evans, who had replaced Sir Percy Cradock as ambassador in Beijing, led the British team. On the Chinese side, Zhou Nan took over from Yao Guang.

Meanwhile, Premier Zhao, while on an official tour of the United States, publicly stated that China would maintain Hong Kong's current social and economic systems for 50 years after it resumes sovereignty in 1997.

Similar assurances were given by Xu Jiatun, director of the Hong Kong branch of the Xinhua news agency. As head of Xinhua, Mr. Xu was China's de facto representative in Hong Kong. His deputy, Li Jusheng, was concurrently deputy head of the Chinese negotiating team. Mr. Xu was sent to Hong Kong in June 1983, while the talks were deadlocked, to take charge of China's affairs in Hong Kong, in particular to strengthen united-front work, that is, to win over people to Beijing's cause. In 1949, Mr. Xu was political commissar of a Communist division that helped to take over Fujian province, across the strait from Taiwan. Before being assigned to Hong Kong, he had been the first party secretary of Jiangsu, China's most prosperous province. Mr. Xu is a member of the Communist party's policymaking Central Committee, the first such high-ranking party official to be named director of Xinhua in Hong Kong. His selection showed the importance Beijing attached to the Hong Kong post, as well as the confidence China's leaders placed in him. While part of Xinhua performed news-gathering and dissemination functions, the job of the more important officials was to represent China's interests in the territory. The director of Xinhua was, in effect, China's high commissioner in the territory.

Hong Kong's apprehension grows

The beginning of 1984 also saw Hong Kong confronting an outbreak of rioting. A taxi drivers' strike raised tensions that led to violence in which 130 people were arrested. The riots reflected the strains within the community and the pressure under which people had been living for so long.

The taxi dispute also brought to the surface another problem that had been worrying the Hong Kong government: that it would be treated as a lame duck government, losing authority and respect long before 1997. A group of striking drivers had approached the Xinhua office in Hong Kong, but China's official representatives wisely decided to stay out of the controversy. However, the danger remains that, as 1997 approaches, other people with grievances will try to go

over the heads of Hong Kong and British officials by appealing directly
to the Chinese government.

With no official representation in the Sino-British negotiations,
Hong Kong residents in general were feeling increasingly frustrated.
The population did not identify with the colonial Hong Kong government, which had always resisted proposals for even a limited form of
representative government. Rather, there was fear that the British, to
safeguard their own relationship with China, might sacrifice the
interests of the Hong Kong populace, about half of whom were
technically British nationals. In 1982, the Hong Kong government had
started introducing a tiny element of democracy by creating District
Boards for each of the territory's 18 districts. Though their function
was purely advisory and two thirds of their members were government
officials or appointees, a third of them were to be directly elected by
voters of each district. The plan was to increase gradually the elected
component of the District Boards, so that democracy could be built
from the bottom up. In addition, the government had proposed setting
up a Regional Council for the New Territories by 1986, with an
extremely limited scope of authority. No reforms were proposed for
making government at the top more representative.

In March, Roger Lobo, a member of the colony's Legislative
Council, suggested that any proposals for the future of Hong Kong
should be debated by the council before a final agreement is reached.
Reaction from the left-wing press was vociferous. The Lobo Motion
was denounced as another attempt to revive the "three-legged stool"
concept and sneak Hong Kong into the negotiations. That same month,
Hong Kong's badly battered sense of confidence was dealt another
blow. Jardine, Matheson and Co., the colony's oldest trading company
and one of the major British establishments in the territory, announced
that it was moving its holding company to Bermuda. That was a clear
vote of no confidence in Hong Kong's future. The next day, the Hang
Seng index plunged nearly 73 points.

British and Chinese bombshells

In April, Sir Geoffrey Howe, the British foreign secretary, visited
Beijing and held high-level discussions with Chinese officials, including Mr. Deng. The talks were described as "warm, friendly and
earnest." Then he flew to Hong Kong and, at a press conference held
on April 20, stunned the colony by officially disclosing for the first time
that Britain had indeed abandoned the fight to retain administrative
control of Hong Kong beyond the expiration of the lease. "It would not
be realistic," he said, "to think of an agreement that provides for
continued British administration in Hong Kong after 1997."

In the wake of the announcement, a shell-shocked group of Execu-

Courtesy of Hong Kong Tourist Association

tive Council (Exco) members, led by Sir S. Y. Chung, flew to London
to appeal to the British government. While Mrs. Thatcher expressed
full understanding of their anxieties, Members of Parliament were less
kind. The visit coincided with a parliamentary debate on the 1997
issue. The Executive Councillors were repeatedly snubbed for not
being representative of the Hong Kong people. This was ironic, since
the British government had never permitted elections in Hong Kong.
They preferred to appoint people they regarded as being representative
of key sectors of the community to the Executive and Legislative
Councils. Now their appointees were being ill-treated by British
M.P.'s because they were not elected.

To counter Exco's poor public image in London, Sir S. Y. Chung, in
a television interview, called on Hong Kong's people to speak up. "If
they don't speak out now, they probably will never have the chance,"
he said. The response was an outpouring of letters and telegrams
voicing support for the Exco delegation.

The people of Hong Kong were worried, suspicious, desperate. In
this atmosphere bordering on hysteria, rumors that Maria's cake shops
were in financial trouble triggered the mindless crowds who lined up
for hours to get cakes.

The following week, another bombshell was dropped—this time by
the Chinese. Mr. Deng, whom many people in Hong Kong trusted
because they viewed him as a moderate, told Hong Kong reporters that,
contrary to what other officials had said, Beijing would definitely
station People's Liberation Army troops in Hong Kong after 1997. The
specter of the People's Liberation Army marching down Hong Kong
streets was an intimidating one, especially since the vast majority of
Hong Kong's population consists of refugees from the Chinese Communists or the children of such refugees.

The die had been cast. Hong Kong's people knew that their lot
would lie with China, not Britain, after 1997. In an attempt to voice the
feelings of Hong Kong, a three-member Exco delegation, led by Sir
S.Y. Chung, went to Beijing. They met Mr. Deng in what many people
regarded as humiliating circumstances. For one thing, Mr. Deng
emphasized he was meeting with them in their status as private
individuals, not representatives of the Executive Council. Moreover, he
implied that they were not Chinese patriots, telling them they should
learn more about "China and the Chinese people."

During the discussion, Mr. Deng made what to Hong Kong's people
was an alarming disclosure: before 1997, China wanted to set up a joint
Sino-British committee in Hong Kong to monitor developments. News
of this caused widespread apprehension that such a panel would
become a stalking horse for China, a means for China to intervene in
Hong Kong affairs long before 1997.

Nonstop negotiations

To step up the pace of negotiations, China and Britain in effect went into permanent session by creating a full-time working group, in addition to the formal negotiating group. On July 27, Sir Geoffrey arrived in Beijing on his second offical visit in three months. Stopping in Hong Kong in early August on his way back to Britain, he announced that substantial progress had been made in the talks and unveiled a 10-point blueprint for Hong Kong. Almost all the points had previously been disclosed by the Chinese, but Sir Geoffrey's presentation made them sound more official. In addition, Sir Geoffrey had soothing news about the Joint Liaison Group proposed by the Chinese. He said that the group would not be "an organ of power," but would only play a liaison role. Moreoever, it would meet alternatively in Beijing, London and Hong Kong, and would only be based in Hong Kong from 1988 on. Lastly, he said the group would continue to function until the year 2000, thus giving the British a role to play beyond 1997. Sir Geoffrey also disclosed that there remained three outstanding issues on which agreement had not been reached: civil aviation, land and nationality.

The announcement of substantial progress provided a psychological shot in the arm for Hong Kong, and the stock market rose 67 points, the largest one-day gain since Prime Minister Thatcher's fateful visit in September 1982.

It was clear that the two sides were getting close to an agreement. Before leaving London for Beijing, Sir Geoffrey had announced to Parliament on July 18 plans to set up a special office in Hong Kong to monitor local reaction to an anticipated draft agreement.

Direct elections?

The Hong Kong government, too, was working frantically to prepare the territory for inevitable changes. In the summer of 1984, it issued a Green Paper on representative government that provided for some members of the Legislative Council to be chosen through elections, albeit indirect ones. (Green Papers provide a guide to official thinking, and offer the public a chance to comment before policies are officially announced in White Papers.) It held out the possibility that, sometime in the future, even direct elections could be considered.

The Green Paper was received without much enthusiasm. The more conservative business community preferred the appointive system, under which many of their members were frequently chosen to serve. Other groups voiced dissatisfaction with the proposed system of indirect elections, calling instead for direct elections. However, the only hope held out by the government was to move forward the date for consideration of the desirability of holding direct elections.

The caution was not only on the British side. China, too, was believed to be skeptical of the wisdom of holding direct elections, whose results were unpredictable. Business people in Hong Kong were fearful that "radicals"—dubbed free-lunchers—would be voted into office.

Joint Declaration: four Chinese concessions

What Sir Geoffrey did not disclose while in Hong Kong were other concessions that China had made during his trip. In addition to modifying the terms of reference of the Joint Liaison Group, the Chinese also consented to four key clauses in the Joint Declaration that Britain had been seeking.

Perhaps the most important of these, from the viewpoint of Hong Kong residents, was a declaration (Paragraph Three, Subsection 12) that bound the Chinese to respect the provisions of the Joint Declaration and Annex I when drafting the Basic Law for Hong Kong. Moreover, those provisions will remain unchanged for 50 years.

Another Chinese concession was the inclusion of a clear statement in the Joint Declaration that Britain will remain responsible for Hong Kong up to 1997 (Paragraph Four).

A third concession, and perhaps the most important one from the British standpoint, was China's acceptance of usage of the word "agree" in the Joint Declaration (Paragraph Seven). The Chinese had wanted Britain to surrender authority over Hong Kong to China, without any Chinese commitment to anything beyond a declaration of their policies toward Hong Kong. Acceptance of the word "agree" meant that Britain could properly call the document an agreement.

The fourth, and last, component of this package was China's agreement to treat the three annexes to the Joint Declaration as being just as binding as the declaration itself. (The first annex is an elaboration by China of its basic policies regarding Hong Kong; the second is on the Sino-British Joint Liaison Group; the third is on land leases.)

Sir Geoffrey did disclose that Britain, despite its earlier rejections of the Chinese deadline, was working to reach an agreement by September. To speed things up, another working group was formed. From then on, the importance of the formal negotiating sessions receded and attention focused on the two working groups, which met daily as the negotiators struggled furiously to meet the Chinese deadline. Language on each issue had to be agreed upon, in both English and Chinese, so that there was no hint of infringement on Chinese sovereignty and, at the same time, as much of the status quo could be preserved as possible. Thus, in describing the future legal system, the drafters basically described the present one, making it clear that no change is envisioned.

The nationality, aviation and land issues

The remaining three formal rounds of negotiations, held in August and early September, were devoted to the three outstanding issues, of which the nationality issue was the most ticklish. Fully half of Hong Kong's population are British nationals, or, technically, British Dependent Territories citizens, who are entitled to travel on British passports, though without the right of abode in Britain. Such passports are much more widely accepted by third countries than those issued by the PRC. If Hong Kong residents can no longer use them after 1997, their freedom to travel may be severely hampered. On the other hand, if China were to recognize the validity of Hong Kong British passports after 1997, it might be seen as an infringement of Chinese sovereignty. There was also the practical problem that half the Hong Kong population might then claim British consular protection.

As the talks on this issue went on, the Chinese adamantly insisted at the negotiating table that, after 1997, the British passport could no longer be used in Hong Kong, or elsewhere in China for that matter. If the records of the negotiations are ever made public, they would disclose no Chinese concession on this matter. However, this is where the informal contacts proved useful. At one of these sessions, the Chinese explained that what they really meant was that, while Hong Kong Chinese would not be recognized as British nationals by China, they would be permitted to continue to travel abroad on British passports, and even to claim British consular protection in foreign countries. In effect, China was agreeing to give them dual nationality.

According to British law, parents can transmit their nationality to their offspring. China, however, insisted that there were limits to what it could tolerate. The privilege of using British passports was therefore confined to the generation born before July 1, 1997.

Because the issue of nationality is so sensitive and touches on the question of sovereignty, the Chinese refused to incorporate it in either the Joint Declaration or its annexes. Instead, the agreement reached is set out in an Exchange of Memoranda by the two governments.

The aviation issue contained serious potential for economic disruption in Hong Kong. China's national airline, CAAC, would undoubtedly love to take over lucrative Hong Kong routes, thus dooming Cathay Pacific, the Hong Kong airline, which is a subsidiary of Swire Pacific Ltd., a major British trading house. Such a move, however, would have given the lie to Chinese promises to maintain prosperity in Hong Kong, and not to intervene in Hong Kong's internal affairs. Thus agreement was reached to permit the continuation of Cathay Pacific. Power to negotiate bilateral air routes was vested in Hong Kong, except for those that terminate in mainland China. Britain, of course, had to give up its right to treat Hong Kong as a domestic British airport: when air service agreements negotiated by Britain expire, they will have to be renegotiated. The British would have to disentangle gradually their air routes from those of Hong Kong.

The last of the sticky issues was that of land. In Hong Kong, all land belongs to the British Crown. The Hong Kong government, by making a certain amount of land available to private industry each year, derives considerable revenue, which in recent years has accounted for 5 to 10 percent of its income. Since the British would yield control of Hong Kong in 1997, they sought China's consent for the current government to continue to offer land leases each year, with the leases running beyond 1997. The Chinese wanted a say on all land leases that extend beyond 1997, but the British balked. The Chinese then proposed that revenue from land be split, with a portion of the revenue being set aside annually in a special fund for the future Special Administrative Region government. The British agreed to a 50–50 split. China's insistence on this measure reflects its continuing distrust of the British and its fear that Britain would siphon off Hong Kong's resources before 1997, leaving China with nothing but a shell.

Talks conclude

The 22nd round of talks was held on September 5 and 6. At the conclusion, no date was announced for the next session. Meetings at the working group level continued. On September 19, China and Britain jointly announced that a draft agreement would be initialed in Beijing the following week.

On September 26, four days before the expiration of the deadline set by China, the Joint Declaration was initialed by Sir Richard Evans, the British ambassador, and Chinese Deputy Foreign Minister Zhou Nan. The two chief negotiators hugged each other awkwardly before they toasted each other with champagne. Sir Percy pursed his lips as if to kiss his Chinese counterpart, but did not make contact.

That afternoon, Sir Edward Youde flew back to Hong Kong by chartered plane and held an extraordinary session of the Legislative Council at 7 p.m. There, the Joint Declaration was presented in the form of a White Paper and made public for the first time. Sir Edward made it clear that, while people in Hong Kong were invited to present their views, not a word of the agreement could be changed. The choice faced by Hong Kong's people was to accept the terms of the secretly negotiated agreement or to have no agreement at all.

Over a million copies of the agreement were printed. They were immediately snapped up, and a new printing had to be ordered. The people of Hong Kong lined up in the middle of the night for copies, so anxious were they to find out the arrangements made for their future.

香港

2
The Agreement

The document several million Hong Kong residents stood in line for was in the form of a 46-page White Paper. Its title, "A Draft Agreement between the Government of the United Kingdom of Great Britain and Northern Ireland and the Government of the People's Republic of China on the Future of Hong Kong," appeared beneath the crest of Hong Kong, which shows the crowned British lion facing the imperial dragon. (See Appendix.)

The White Paper was in four parts: An Introduction, the Joint Declaration and its three Annexes, an Exchange of Memoranda, and Explanatory Notes. The Introduction and the Explanatory Notes are not part of the agreement but are statements by the British government providing background information and some interpretation.

The Introduction sketches the history of Hong Kong from the time it first came under British rule in 1842, in the aftermath of the Opium War, and ends with the course of the two-year-long negotiations. It also makes the claim that the agreement is "legally binding" on Britain and China, and says in bold face: "Her Majesty's government believe that the agreement is a good one. They strongly commend it to the people of Hong Kong and to Parliament." The Introduction ends with an invitation to the people of Hong Kong "to comment on the overall acceptability of the draft agreement on Hong Kong," but, as noted in an earlier paragraph, "the alternative to acceptance of the present agreement is to have no agreement."

The Chinese government, like the British, distributed copies of the agreement in both English and Chinese. The version the Chinese distributed, however, contains only the agreement, without benefit of Introduction or Explanatory Notes. Moreover, while the British White Paper is called a "Draft Agreement" on the "Future" of Hong Kong, the Chinese-distributed version gives it its proper name—a "Joint Declaration" by the two governments on the "Question" of Hong Kong.

China's Foreign Minister Wu Xueqian, in a report on November 6, 1984, to the standing committee of the National People's Congress, explained the Chinese government's position on Hong Kong: "Generally speaking, territorial and sovereign matters between nations are mainly handled by treaties. However, in consideration of the fact that our government's basic principles and policies on Hong Kong involve our country's internal affairs, such principles and policies should be declared by our side. In the meantime, it would be more appropriate to adopt the form of a 'joint declaration' to handle the questions of sovereignty and administrative rights. The details concerned shall be explained in the form of an appendix. Of course, in a broader sense, a 'joint declaration' is also a form of international treaty, which has the force of international law and legal binding power at the same time."

Similarly, determining the "future" of Hong Kong would be considered by Beijing to be an internal Chinese matter that need not concern Britain. However, resumption of the exercise of Chinese sovereignty over the British Crown Colony is a "question" that requires negotiations between the two governments. Such nicety in the choice of words indicates a degree of sensitivity on the part of at least the PRC government, and probably the British government as well.

The Joint Declaration itself consists of eight numbered paragraphs. In Paragraph One, China declares its intention to "resume the exercise of sovereignty over Hong Kong with effect from 1 July 1997." In Paragraph Two, Britain declares that it will "restore Hong Kong to the PRC with effect from 1 July 1997."

These two paragraphs set the tone of the whole document, which is truly a joint declaration, with each party declaring its intentions. Of course, taken together, the joint declarations dovetail into an agreement. But, by having China and Britain make separate declarations about their intentions, awkward and divisive conflicts are avoided. Thus, the two sides were able to finesse the delicate issue of whether the three 19th-century treaties are valid, as Britain has contended, or "null and void," which has always been China's position.

Paragraph Three: China's 12 points

The heart of the agreement (Paragraph Three) is a 12-point declaration by China of its intended policies toward Hong Kong after 1997. Though none of the points are new or surprising, it does represent the first time that China has asserted solemnly in an international agreement that Hong Kong's social and economic systems and lifestyle will remain basically unchanged for 50 years after 1997, with the territory to be run by local inhabitants and not by officials sent from Beijing.

In brief, the 12 points call for turning Hong Kong into a Special Administrative Region of the PRC, with a high degree of autonomy except in foreign affairs and defense. An impressive list of rights and freedoms is guaranteed. And Hong Kong's status as a free port and as an international financial center is to be maintained.

The 12 points conclude with a pledge by China that the basic policies of the PRC regarding Hong Kong and its elaboration of them in Annex I will be stipulated in a Basic Law.

The next four paragraphs are declarations jointly made by the two governments. Britain and China agree that, until June 30, 1997, the United Kingdom will be responsible for the administration of Hong Kong. This statement is historic in that for the first time since the birth of the PRC, Beijing is openly legitimizing foreign rule over a part of what it claims to be Chinese territory, though only for a period of 13 years.

Paragraph Seven is important in that it is the only place in the entire text where the word "agree" appears, allowing the British to call it an "agreement." The two governments "agree to implement the preceding declarations and the annexes to this Joint Declaration."

Paragraph Eight, which concludes the Joint Declaration, states that it shall come into force "on the date of the exchange of instruments of ratification, which shall take place in Beijing before 30 June 1985. This Joint Declaration and its annexes shall be equally binding." This last sentence has stirred some controversy for, while it says the annexes are binding, it makes no mention of the "Exchange of Memoranda." The memoranda deal with the important issue of nationality.

The governor of Hong Kong, Sir Edward Youde, was asked at a news conference on September 27, 1984, the day after the initialing of the agreement, why "such an important issue as the nationality issue [is] covered in the form of a memorandum . . . which is not legally binding. . . ." Sir Edward's response did not touch on whether the memoranda are legally binding. Instead, he said: "Each of these subjects is dealt with in the form in which the governments felt it was best dealt with, and the fact that it is in an exchange of memoranda does not in any way mean that it is not regarded as an important one. On the contrary, there was an immense amount of attention and care given to devising this very practical answer to a practical problem."

Sir Edward was pressed by another reporter to expand on his reply. "I notice that you skirted various questions on nationality over the course of the press conference," the reporter said. "Surely the fact that the nationality issue is treated in a memorandum is because it is not part of the agreement. It is not part of the agreement because both sides have agreed to disagree; and Britain has to make the best of what is essentially a bad job in that area."

The governor replied: "No, I think what has happened is that both sides have agreed to agree on a practical arrangement which takes account of the positions of both sides. There is in that exchange of memoranda a very practical arrangement which gives those who will be affected, the British Dependent Territories citizens, a new status which will allow them to travel as they would wish, or as many would wish, on British passports, and the same arrangements still give people in Hong Kong a right of abode. So, far from being an agreement to disagree it seems to me specifically an agreement to agree on a practical arrangement."

Annex I: government

Of the three annexes to the Joint Declaration, Annex I is by far the longest—four times the length of the Joint Declaration itself. It is an elaboration by the Chinese government of its basic policies regarding Hong Kong, which are set forth in Paragraph Three of the Joint Declaration.

At the beginning of Annex I, Section I, the Chinese government cites Article 31 of the Chinese constitution as justification for establishing a Hong Kong Special Administrative Region. Accordingly, it says, as of July 1, 1997, Hong Kong will become a Special Administrative Region of the PRC, and the National People's Congress "shall enact and promulgate a Basic Law. . . ." (This Basic Law is occasionally referred to in Hong Kong as the territory's "mini-constitution.") The Basic Law will stipulate that "the socialist system and socialist policies shall not be practiced . . . and that Hong Kong's previous capitalist system and lifestyle shall remain unchanged for 50 years."

Annex I places Hong Kong directly under the authority of the central government in Beijing, which shall authorize it to conduct its own internal affairs as well as certain external affairs. Significantly, it also asserts that the Hong Kong legislature "shall be constituted by elections," though the form of the elections was not spelled out. The annex also says that both Chinese and English may be used by government organs and by the courts, and allows Hong Kong to display a regional flag and emblem in addition to the national flag and emblem of the PRC.

Law and justice

On legislation, Annex I, Section II, says that "laws previously in force . . . shall be maintained, save for any that contravene the Basic Law and subject to any amendment by the Hong Kong Special Administrative Region legislature." All laws enacted by the Hong Kong legislature are to be reported to the Standing Committee of China's National People's Congress "for the record" and those "which are in accordance with the Basic Law and legal procedures shall be regarded as valid." It is unclear whether the National People's Congress will have to make a judgment on each individual piece of legislation and, if so, whether it is up to the congress to pronounce on the validity of each proposed law.

As to the judicial system, Annex I, Section III, provides that "the judicial system previously practiced in Hong Kong shall be maintained except for those changes consequent upon the vesting in the courts of the Hong Kong Special Administrative Region of the power of final adjudication." Under British rule, the power of such final adjudication has been with the Privy Council in London. Such power is to be transferred to Hong Kong itself, not to Beijing, after 1997.

Judges are to be appointed by the Hong Kong chief executive, according to "the recommendation of an independent commission composed of local judges, persons from the legal profession and other eminent persons." Foreigners, or "judges from other common law jurisdictions," may be recruited to serve in Hong Kong. Foreign judges may also be invited to sit on the court of final appeal. Similarly, foreign lawyers will be allowed to practice in Hong Kong. This, in effect, is a description of the present system.

Criminal prosecutions are to be controlled by a "prosecuting authority of the Hong Kong Special Administrative Region" and are to be "free from any interference." This provision is one that representatives of Hong Kong legal circles had been pressing for.

Civil service

Annex I, Section IV, provides that civil servants will have continuity of employment and guarantees their pension rights. The future Hong Kong government will also be free to employ "British and other foreign nationals . . . at all levels, except as heads of major government departments (corresponding to branches or departments at secretary level) including the police department, and as deputy heads of some of those departments." In addition, British and other foreign nationals may be employed as advisers or appointed to professional and technical posts in government departments. Significantly, the annex adds that foreign nationals are to be employed only in their individual capacities.

As for financial matters (Section V), the Hong Kong Special Administrative Region will have autonomy in the allocation of its financial resources and in drawing up its budgets and its final accounts. Budgets and final accounts are to be reported to the central government "for the record." There is no implication that approval of the central government will be required. All revenues raised in Hong Kong are to be used exclusively by Hong Kong and not handed over to Beijing.

Capitalism and free trade assured

The Hong Kong Special Administrative Region is also given great latitude in economic matters: it "shall maintain the capitalist economic and trade systems previously practiced in Hong Kong," Section VI of the annex says. Hong Kong is to remain a free port, continue a free-trade policy and may take part in international organizations and international trade agreements, such as GATT.

Control of the monetary and financial systems, too, is to be retained. Annex I, Section VII, says the Hong Kong Special Administrative Region may decide on monetary and financial policies. It also says that no exchange-control policy is to be applied in Hong Kong. (Whether this means the Hong Kong Special Administrative Region government will not have the right to impose such controls if one day it deems them necessary is unclear.) The local currency is to remain freely convertible, and the currency is to be issued by banks designated by the Hong Kong Special Administrative Region. (At present, the Hong Kong and Shanghai Banking Corporation and the Chartered Bank are the only ones authorized to issue currency.)

Shipping and aviation

On shipping, Annex I, Section VIII, calls for the maintenance of the present systems of shipping management and shipping regulation. However, access to Hong Kong harbor by foreign warships will require the permission of the PRC. At present, ships of the U.S. Seventh Fleet call periodically at the colony, so that sailors can enjoy a period of "rest and recreation." It is unclear if the PRC will permit these visits to continue after 1997.

The next issue dealt with (Section IX) is the sensitive and controversial matter of aviation. The issue impinges on sovereignty, since the British government has treated Hong Kong International Airport as a domestic British airport, and traded landing rights in Hong Kong for the right of British airlines to service other countries. If China were to extend the monopoly of its national airline, CAAC, to Hong Kong, it could effectively put Hong Kong's airline, Cathay Pacific, out of business. The agreement reached, however, grants Hong Kong considerable latitude. It provides for the continuation of the previous system of civil aviation management in Hong Kong with Hong Kong keeping "its own aircraft register in accordance with provisions laid down by the Central People's government. . . ." While the central government is to make all agreements governing air service to and from Hong Kong, the special conditions and economic interests of Hong Kong will be taken into consideration, and the Special Administrative Region government shall be consulted.

The system of education (Section X) previously practiced in Hong Kong is to be maintained. The Special Administrative Region government can decide its own policies and set the language of instruction. Church-run schools may continue to function. Staff and teaching materials from foreign countries may be employed.

Foreign and consular relations

Although foreign affairs are the responsibility of the PRC, Annex I, Section XI, states that representatives of the Hong Kong Special Administrative Region government may participate as members of delegations of the PRC government in negotiations directly affecting Hong Kong. In addition, using the name "Hong Kong, China," the Special Administrative Region may on its own "maintain and develop relations and conclude and implement agreements with states, regions and relevant international organizations in . . . the economic, trade, financial and monetary, shipping, communications, touristic, cultural and sporting fields." Hong Kong may also participate in international organizations (such as the Asian Development Bank), whose membership is not limited to states.

As for consulates in Hong Kong, of which there are many right now, those from countries with which China has diplomatic relations may be maintained unchanged. Those from countries with which China has no diplomatic relations may "either be maintained or changed to semiofficial missions. States not recognized by the PRC can only establish nongovernmental institutions."

The consulate issue is important from a practical standpoint since many of Hong Kong's trading partners do not have diplomatic relations with China. They include South Korea, Singapore, Saudi Arabia, Indonesia, Taiwan, South Africa and Israel. If Hong Kong is to remain a major center of commerce and finance after 1997, it would be important for its international standing not to be eroded. But a large-scale closing down of consulates would certainly have that effect, and might even impair the ability of Hong Kong people to travel freely.

Privately, however, Chinese officials have indicated that the only countries that would not be allowed to maintain consulates in Hong Kong after 1997 are South Korea, Israel and South Africa. The Chinese have pointed out that the Vienna convention of 1815, which set forth rules of diplomacy that are still in effect, states that consular relations do not necessarily imply diplomatic relations. Moreover, it is entirely possible that by 1997 China will have normalized its relations with some of these countries. Already Singapore, which has no diplomatic relations with China, has a trade office in Beijing, and agreement on direct flights between China and Singapore has been reached. Indonesia suspended diplomatic relations with China in the 1960s, but relations between the two countries are becoming friendlier. Indonesia extended and China accepted an invitation to attend celebrations in April 1985 marking the 30th anniversary of the Bandung Conference of nonaligned nations. The three politically sensitive countries mentioned above will probably be permitted to set up trade offices. Taiwan is the main problematic area. China has called on Taiwan to maintain its trade and other relations with Hong Kong after 1997, but Taiwan's attitude remains unclear.

Under Annex I, Section XII, maintenance of public order is the responsibility of the Special Administrative Region government. Troops sent by the central government to be stationed in Hong Kong, the section says, shall not interfere in internal affairs.

Rights and freedoms

An impressive array of rights and freedoms of the inhabitants of Hong Kong is to be protected by the Special Administrative Region government under Section XIII. Some of these rights are also embodied in the Chinese constitution while others, such as freedom to choose one's occupation or the right to raise a family, are not.

Annex I also spells out the right to freedom of religion, a right also guaranteed under the Chinese constitution. But a significant difference between the right of individuals on the mainland and in Hong Kong is that, in the Special Administrative Region, "religious organizations and believers may maintain their relations with religious organizations and believers elsewhere. . . ." This clause is of special importance to the Roman Catholic Church in Hong Kong, which will be allowed to maintain ties with Rome. The Catholic Church in China was forced to sever its ties with the Vatican after the Communist takeover.

People with the right of abode in Hong Kong are defined in Annex I, Section XIV, as "all Chinese nationals who were born or who have ordinarily resided in Hong Kong . . . for a continuous period of seven years or more, and persons of Chinese nationality born outside Hong Kong of such Chinese nationals," as well as "persons who have ordinarily resided in Hong Kong . . . for a continuous period of seven years or more and who have taken Hong Kong as their place of permanent residence. . . ."

Joint Liaison Group

Annex II concerns the Sino-British Joint Liaison Group. The establishment of such a group, proposed by the Chinese, was viewed with great suspicion by segments of the Hong Kong community, who saw it as offering China a means to intervene in local affairs before 1997. However, Sir Geoffrey Howe, after discussions with Mr. Deng, was able to state categorically that such a group, to be formed when the Joint Declaration comes into effect, "will not be an organ of power."

As defined by Annex II, the purpose of the Joint Liaison Group is liaison, consultation and the exchange of information between Britain and China.

Since the liaison group's terms of reference are broadly defined, it is actually in a position to tackle any problem that may arise between now and 1997, since it will not cease to exist until 2000. The liaison group certainly offers a channel for China to influence events and policies in Hong Kong before 1997, just as it offers Britain a similar avenue for two and a half years after 1997.

Annex III is the last part of the agreement proper. It deals with the subject of land leases. This annex gives the present Hong Kong British government the right to give or renew leases on land up to June 30, 2047. Such leases are to be recognized by the future Special Administrative Region government. However, the annex places a ceiling of 50 hectares on new land that may be made available by the Hong Kong government each year from the entry into force of the Joint Declaration until June 30, 1997. Moreover, "premium income obtained by the British Hong Kong government from land transactions shall, after deduction of the average cost of land production, be shared equally between the British Hong Kong government and the future Hong Kong Special Administrative Region government."

This annex also provides for the establishment of a Land Commission, composed of Chinese and British officials, which shall monitor the observance of the limit of new land made available each year. The establishment of the Land Commission is an indication of China's apprehension that Britain may sell off all choice land and fritter away the territory's assets before 1997.

Nationality and travel

Following the Joint Declaration and the three annexes is the Exchange of Memoranda on the subject of nationality and travel documents. Currently, approximately half of the 5.5 million residents of

Hong Kong are eligible for British Dependent Territories passports. Such passports find greater acceptance elsewhere than do passports of the PRC, and hence facilitate travel by Hong Kong business people and tourists. After 1997, however, Hong Kong's people will no longer be British Dependent Territories citizens. The two memoranda represent an attempt by Britain to give current British Dependent Territories citizens a special status, even after 1997, and China's acquiescence. Even the current British Dependent Territories passport does not entitle its holder to right of abode in Britain, only in Hong Kong.

The British memorandum declares that all persons who on June 30, 1997, are British Dependent Territories citizens will be "eligible to retain an appropriate status which, without conferring the right of abode in the United Kingdom, will entitle them to continue to use passports issued by the government of the United Kingdom." The British memorandum envisages a new status for such people, a status that currently does not exist.

The Chinese memorandum, prepared in response to the British memorandum, states without ambiguity that under Chinese law "all Hong Kong Chinese compatriots, whether they are holders of the 'British Dependent Territories citizens' passports' or not, are Chinese nationals."

However, it says that, taking into consideration the historical background of Hong Kong and its realities, the Chinese government will, after July 1, 1997, "permit Chinese nationals in Hong Kong who were previously called 'British Dependent Territories citizens' to use travel documents issued by the government of the United Kingdom for the purpose of traveling to other states and regions." But, it warns, such Chinese nationals "will not be entitled to British consular protection in the Hong Kong Special Administrative Region and other parts of the PRC." The memorandum carefully avoids using the word "passports"—which may be thought to confer nationality—preferring the term "travel documents." Its intent clearly is to allow such people to use British-issued travel documents and to permit recourse to British consular protection in third countries—that is, countries other than the PRC or Britain.

In effect, holders of post-1997 British-issued passports will be in an extraordinary position. While in Hong Kong or China, they will be considered Chinese citizens. They will have no right of abode in Britain. Yet, when traveling in third countries, they will in effect have dual nationality, being able to enjoy British consular protection. British nationality laws permit citizenship to be transmitted to children of British citizens. China, however, was adamant in insisting that the right to hold British travel documents will end with this generation. Britain acquiesced.

In the spring of 1983, the British government disclosed that the new status of British Dependent Territories citizen will be known as British National (Overseas). The British pledged to seek third-country acceptance of the new passport. However, since such passport holders will not have the right of abode in Britain, it is unclear how persuasive Britain will be. Holders of the new British National (Overseas) passport will theoretically not be able to prove that they have the right of abode anywhere. Under these circumstances, immigration authorities may look askance at the holder of such a passport. The suggestion has been made that people who travel on such passports carry with them Hong Kong identity cards.

The British-issued White Paper concludes with 12 pages of Explanatory Notes, which provide background information and attempt to clarify ambiguity and expand on the ramifications of statements. For example, the notes point out that Annex I means that Hong Kong will "not be under the authority of any provincial government," a matter that has been of concern to some people who fear interference in Hong Kong affairs not by Beijing but, for example, by officials of neighboring Guangdong province.

Although the Introduction and the Explanatory Notes do not form part of the agreement, the British cleared them with Chinese officials, so presumably the Chinese government does not quarrel with the British interpretation of the document.

Hong Kong's reaction

Most people who took part in public discussions found the agreement much more detailed, and more reassuring, than they had expected. One feature of the Joint Declaration, however, that many Hong Kong residents are unhappy about is its reference to the stationing of Chinese troops in Hong Kong. Several Chinese leaders had said troops would not be sent, and some Hong Kong residents see China's reversal on this issue as a sign that it may also renege on other commitments.

Missing from the Joint Declaration is a statement as to whether China will conscript Hong Kong youths to serve in the armed forces. The British pressed for a declaration, and the Chinese said their policy was not to draft men from Hong Kong. But they refused to incorporate such a pledge in the Joint Declaration. Taken as a whole, however, the agreement—in all its detail and the care with which it was negotiated—signaled China's desire to reassure Hong Kong residents of its intention to abide by it.

But the Joint Declaration is only the first step. The crucial next step is the drafting of the Basic Law. In the process, it is important that there be no dilution of the Joint Declaration's principles.

The Basic Law will have to define such matters as citizenship. It will also have to take account of the sizable nonethnic Chinese minorities in Hong Kong, including some 6,000 Indians who hold British Dependent Territories citizenship and up to 100,000 Vietnamese refugees who may have nowhere else to go.

The manner in which the Hong Kong government is to be formed, including how the chief executive is to be chosen, will also have to be spelled out. The Joint Declaration is vague about this, saying merely that China will appoint a chief executive who is chosen as a result of consultation or election. The scope of the legislature's authority and how its members are to be elected also needs to be defined.

Another serious problem is whether the right to interpret the Basic Law resides with the National People's Congress in Beijing or the Hong Kong courts. In China, the congress not only adopts but also interprets the constitution, and China may well assert its right to interpret the Basic Law as well. This is a potential source of conflict between Beijing and Hong Kong.

The Joint Declaration, despite its shortcomings, provides for the maintenance of all those elements that have contributed to Hong Kong's success, except for the British link. Apparently, none of these provisions were difficult to negotiate, since China's stand from the beginning was that it would preserve the status quo in Hong Kong— minus the British administration. But China's initial demand that the Joint Liaison Group be an organ of power is sobering, as are statements by high Chinese officials that Hong Kong should not fear intervention by Beijing as long as it is "good intervention" rather than "bad intervention." In the last analysis, the value of the Joint Declaration depends on China's willingness and ability to abide by its letter and its spirit.

香港

3

The Future:
View from Hong Kong

Two weeks after the Sino-British agreement was initialed, this author was talking to a local businessman and the conversation turned to the future of Hong Kong. The businessman said he thought the terms of the agreement were "too good" to be believable. "If I were looking for a job, and I know that I'm worth $30,000, but they offer me $60,000, I'd think there was something fishy," he said. Incredibly, while previously many people feared the agreement would not give Hong Kong sufficient autonomy, once an agreement was reached, these people found other reasons to be apprehensive. These new fears were but another manifestation of the deep-seated distrust that many people in Hong Kong have of the Chinese Communists, a distrust born of their own experience in China and of events on the mainland.

Hong Kong and China have been growing in different directions for more than three decades. Ever since the British took over the colony 140 years ago, China has been wracked by strife, including foreign invasions, civil wars and warlordism, culminating in the Communist-Nationalist struggle. During all this time, the British presence acted as a buffer, preventing Hong Kong from being dragged into the Chinese political maelstrom. In fact, prominent Chinese political figures, including Sun Yat-sen, known as the father of the Revolution, who died in 1925, and Zhou Enlai, China's No. 2 leader until his death in 1976, sought refuge in the British colony.

The British are certainly aware of the widespread distrust of the Communists on the part of the Hong Kong population, and undoubtedly share it to some extent. That may be why, after the draft agreement was initialed, they did everything possible to mute public misgivings. The British made it clear that there was no real alternative for Hong Kong but to accept the agreement as negotiated.

Under these circumstances, Hong Kong's acquiescence was a foregone conclusion. And with the people of Hong Kong having bestowed their blessings on the agreement, its ratification by the British Parliament became a mere formality.

Sir S.Y. Chung, the senior unofficial, or appointed, member of the Executive Council—who had been humiliated in both London and Beijing when he attempted to plead Hong Kong's case—issued a statement on September 28, 1984. Speaking for the other members as well, he said: "It is our belief that what we have today is the best agreement possible and one which we, the unofficial members of the Executive Council, can commend to the people of Hong Kong in good conscience. The world at large will observe the good faith with which it is being implemented and we trust the people of Hong Kong can also take heart from this."

Despite this, Sir S.Y. Chung and his colleagues made another trip to London to lobby British parliamentarians on the eve of the debate by the House of Commons and the House of Lords. Before their departure, they issued the following statement:

> While the draft agreement is acceptable as a whole to the majority of the community, some concern and points of detail have been raised. In particular, there is anxiety about interference from the Chinese government; worry about conscription in the Hong Kong Special Administrative Region; uncertainty about the acceptability to third countries of the new form of British passport; doubt about the preservation of existing human rights and personal freedoms; fear about the stationing of People's Liberation Army troops in Hong Kong; resentment about termination of transmissibility of British nationality for Hong Kong BDTCs [British Dependent Territories citizens] in 1997; reservations about possible incompatibility between the constitution of the PRC and the future Basic Law of Hong Kong; and concern about the faithful implementation of the agreement and the policies of future Chinese leaders.

Sir S.Y. Chung and his colleagues pleaded: "In accepting the agreement, we urge both the British and Chinese governments to take steps to reassure people of Hong Kong in these respects."

Hong Kong 'plebiscite'

The British, despite earlier reservations, had to accommodate this concern. They established an Assessment Office in Hong Kong to receive submissions from the public. Advertisements on television and in the newspapers asked the public to write to the Assessment Office as to whether, taken as a package, the agreement was acceptable. The advertisements gave no indication that the Assessment Office was interested in any "buts" that respondents might have. Clearly, however, there were people with reservations.

As soon as the Assessment Office was set up, questions were raised as to whether the submissions made by members of the public would be kept confidential. No provision had been made for this. Instead, the Assessment Office had insisted that all submissions had to be accompanied by the person's name and address, and that anonymous submissions would be discarded. When the issue of confidentiality was raised in the Legislative Council, the Hong Kong government responded that all submissions would be sent to London, where they would be kept under lock and key for 30 years, after which they might be made public. This, far from having a soothing influence, provoked further agitation. Many people realized that, 30 years from now, they would be living as Chinese nationals on Chinese soil. Anything they put down in writing in 1984 might come back to haunt them in the year 2014. Therefore they wanted all submissions destroyed once they had been processed.

The government could see that unless corrective action was taken the Assessment Office could have been embarrassed by a dearth of responses. Hurried consultations took place between Hong Kong and London, ending with the promise by the government that all submissions would be kept in Hong Kong and destroyed in 1985 when the agreement went into effect.

In addition, the British, without actually acknowledging it, altered the terms of reference of the Assessment Office. In mid-October, the British foreign secretary said in London that, while the agreement itself could not be amended, it could in effect be supplemented. Suggestions that Hong Kong's people have for improving it, he said, would be useful in Britain's future dealings with China. As a result, the Assessment Office amended its newspaper advertisements and asked members of the public not only whether the agreement was acceptable but for "any other views" that they might have.

A 'postdated check'

When the Assessment Office released the report of its findings at the end of November—just in time for the British parliamentary debate on Hong Kong—it came as no surprise to anyone that its main conclusion was the following: "After the most careful analysis and consideration of all the information received, the office has concluded that most of the people of Hong Kong find the draft agreement acceptable. . . ."

"The proposition that an agreement between Britain and China on the future of Hong Kong is preferable to there being no agreement is generally understood and accepted. Furthermore, although anxieties and reservations have been expressed by many, . . . the detailed provisions of the draft agreement have been welcomed. . . ."

As one person who wrote to the Assessment Office said: "It is difficult to foresee the future. The draft agreement is a postdated check. The result can only be known when it is proved."

A feeling of resentment and futility is apparent in the responses of other people, such as the author of the following:

> I belong to the middle income group who do not have the means to emigrate to other countries, and because I was born and educated in Hong Kong, I would wish to stay in Hong Kong. For the purpose of your statistics you can classify me as one of those who would accept the draft agreement, but I hope you will also take into account that I only accept it with much reluctance and with many reservations about the feasibility of its implementation. My heart is not truly at ease and I have no full confidence in our future. The whole thing has not been a very fair play to us because we have not had any say and there is no alternative other than not to have an agreement at all.

There was also a sense of having been let down by the British, especially on the part of naturalized British citizens. One man wrote: "This British government ought to have compassion for those people who fled the cruelties of Communist China to Hong Kong so as to assist in resettling them elsewhere." Another said: "Britain cannot simply rescind a historic and moral responsibility of looking after her subjects. These people are legally British and cannot be made stateless."

"With one stroke of the pen, you have stripped us of our identity and slotted us into racial categories—an unforgivable act, . . ." was the way one letter writer excoriated the British. Another pointed out the irony of having had to swear allegiance to the British monarch when he was naturalized: "I feel the oath of allegiance to the Queen to be very serious and am disillusioned by what the British government has done."

Perhaps the strongest condemnation of Britain came from an appointed member of the Legislative Council, John Swaine, who said that Britain "disabled itself a long time ago, when it closed the door to Hong Kong . . . by a series of immigration and nationality acts which turned the Hong Kong-passport holder into a second-class citizen."

Even more disillusioned than Mr. Swaine was T.S. Lo, a long-time member of both the Executive and Legislative councils and scion of a distinguished Hong Kong family. Mr. Lo did not even speak during the Legislative Council debate on the agreement and resigned in protest from both councils, the first such resignation in the colony's history. The resignation, submitted in October after the Joint Declaration was initialed, was not announced by the government until February 1985, long after the Hong Kong accord had been approved by the British Parliament. Mr. Lo, in an interview, said that he was not prepared to work with the British because of their "total failure to meet their responsibility to their nationals": they had systematically eliminated for British nationals in Hong Kong the right of abode in Britain. "Their only interest is whether people are going to be dumped on their doorstep," he said. "I have no personal disappointment. They haven't betrayed me. I've got a British passport. But 2 million people have been betrayed." To assist people who may wish to emigrate from Hong Kong, Mr. Lo contributed HK$500,000 to help set up a nonprofit organization, called Hong Kong Freedom of Movement and Rights of Abode Ltd., to provide information on immigration matters around the world.

Long before the setting up of the Assessment Office, opinion polls carried out in 1982 made it clear that the vast majority of the population preferred the status quo. The polls also showed differences among various age groups. One poll, for instance, disclosed that while one third of the people in the 45–60 age group considered their roots to be in China, 65 percent of the general population considered their roots to be in Hong Kong. And while 57 percent of the respondents said they would emigrate if they had a chance, 70 percent of those in the 15-24 age group said they would do so. This desire of the younger generation to emigrate does not bode well for the future.

Calm before the storm

The draft agreement did at least one thing for Hong Kong. It restored calm to the community. Many people decided to try to make as much money in Hong Kong as possible before finally leaving, while others could not afford to wait a dozen years. Some people in their 30s and 40s felt that if they had to start a new life in a strange land, it was better to do so as soon as possible. But even people confronted with such decisions no longer discussed them in public. The time had come for action, not talk.

A 40-year-old man who ran his own company figured that he still had two or three years in which to observe developments in Hong Kong. After that time, his children would be near college age, and he would not be able to postpone a decision about where they should get their education. Sending children to study abroad is often a form of insurance for the parents; if the children settle down overseas, the parents can join them later. Another man, a lawyer, said his wife and their children were already living in San Francisco, where he had bought a house. He was remaining in Hong Kong for the time being but had put his house on the market. He could not publicly disclose his planned departure from Hong Kong, he said, or he would be struck off the rolls by the Law Society.

So many people have taken steps to give themselves an option to emigrate eventually that a new vocabulary has developed mostly based on Chinese puns. A "spaceman," or *tai-kong-ren,* is a man (*ren*) who is living alone because his *tai-tai,* or wife, is *kong,* or has gone abroad. Punning on the word *mei,* which can mean both beautiful and America, and the traditional Chinese term for wife and husband—*nei* and *wai,* meaning the person who stays inside the house and the person who goes out—a man whose wife has moved to the United States is described as having "inner beauty," while a woman whose husband has emigrated to America is said to have "outer beauty." The play on words extended to both the Chinese-speaking and English-speaking communities. Stringing together the last names of British Foreign Secretary Sir Geoffrey Howe, Governor Sir Edward Youde, and the principal Foreign Office person responsible for Hong Kong affairs, Richard Luce, resulted in Howe Youde Luce Hong Kong.

One anonymous pundit with a sense of humor composed a new version of the Lord's Prayer, which went:

> Our brother which art in Beijing
> Xiaoping be thy name
> United Kingdom gone
> Thy will be done in here as it is in the Forbidden City
> Give us this day our daily bet
> And forgive us our speculations
> As we forgive them that speculate against us
> Lead us not into communism
> But deliver us from the Gweilos
> For thine is the Sovereignty, the Power and the Territory
> Forever and ever, Amen.

Gweilo is the commonly used Cantonese term for foreigners, which literally means "ghosts."

Other segments of the community found China's formula of "one country, two systems," with Hong Kong people themselves being entrusted to run the territory, very attractive. They had little love for the British anyway. They, too, are taking action, preparing for the day when they can be masters in their own home, with the stigma of colonialism and imperialism removed.

The majority of Hong Kong's people appear resigned to the lot that fate has handed them. In any event, most people do not want to or cannot leave Hong Kong: as Chinese, they favor the ending of the colonial status, but they have lingering doubts about the Communists' willingness or ability to honor their pledges. Such people generally are taking a wait-and-see attitude.

Hong Kong's Chinese identity

It is important to differentiate between fear of the Communists and an identification with Chinese traditions, Chinese culture and the Chinese people as a nation. Even the most rabid anti-Communist Chinese in Hong Kong would find it difficult to argue that sovereignty over the territory should not belong to China. There may be arguments over the legitimacy or the merits of the government in power in China, but not over whether Hong Kong rightfully belongs to China.

For this reason, it is entirely possible for the gulf that now separates Hong Kong from the mainland to be narrowed gradually over the next dozen years. In fact, the nationalistic feelings of Hong Kong's people are likely to increase as China becomes stronger and takes its place among the major powers of the world. Pride in the achievements of China will foster greater identification of Hong Kong with Beijing before the territory's formal reversion. On October 1, 1984, when a massive military parade was held in Beijing to mark the 35th anniversary of the People's Republic of China, the spectacle was covered live on Hong Kong television. The sight undoubtedly bolstered feelings of nationalism among many people who ordinarily devote little thought to politics.

Economic priorities, political necessities

From the viewpoint of the average Hong Kong person, then, the most important thing now is to make the agreement work. It is necessary to see to it that the economy continues to function well, both for Hong Kong and for China, while at the same time gradually instituting political reforms.

In this regard, it is encouraging that the economy has been doing well in recent months. It is perhaps incredible that puny Hong Kong, whose primary natural resource is its people, chalked up a total trade in 1983 of $46 billion (U.S.), including reexports, while the total trade of mighty China with its 1 billion people amounted to somewhat less, $42.4 billion. Figures for 1984 are comparable, with China's trade amounting to $50 billion, while that of Hong Kong, including reexports, exceeded $57 billion.

The high export levels Hong Kong has enjoyed since the second quarter of 1983 are primarily a reflection of the world economic recov-

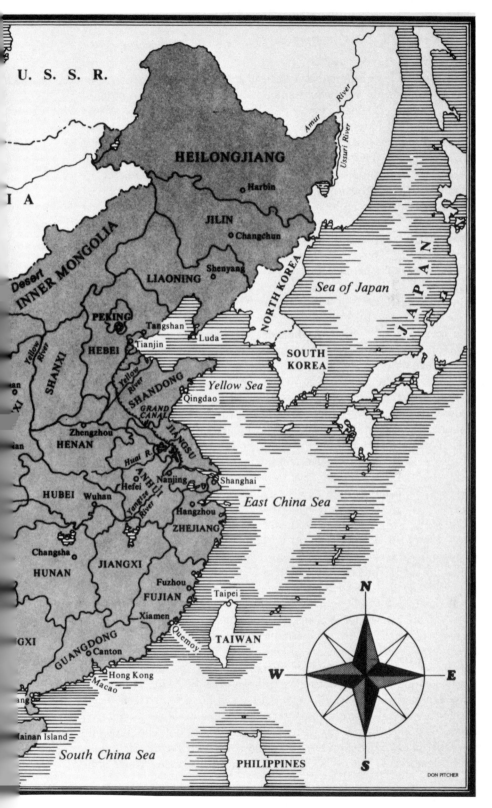

From *China: Alive in the Bitter Sea* by Fox Butterfield. © 1982 by Fox Butterfield.
Reprinted by permission of Times Books, a division of Random House, Inc.

ery. Investment in equipment in 1982 and 1983 was stagnant, when the business community was deeply anxious about the future. Imports of capital goods also declined, clearly reflecting business anxiety.

The growth of Hong Kong's exports in 1984 was a very respectable 17 percent, with a low 3.9 percent rate of unemployment in the last quarter. Inflation slowed to 4.6 percent in December 1984, down from 12.4 percent in January. By the spring of 1985, there had been a noticeable revival in business confidence and reinvestment on the part of local manufacturers, which is far more important to the Hong Kong economy than foreign investment. The Hong Kong government, China and Britain all sounded upbeat in their public pronouncements. The same is true of people in the private sector. By voicing optimism about the future, businessmen are at least making it more likely that the next few years under British rule will be prosperous. The Joint Declaration, at the very least, has bought Hong Kong a little more time. Even the pessimists now think they have at least five more years in which to make money, after which, if they deem it wise, they can look for greener pastures. For the short term at least, the outlook for Hong Kong is good. And, if the Hong Kong Special Administrative Region is to be a success after 1997, it is imperative that the territory be stable and prosperous in the next 12 years. If Hong Kong's prosperity should decline well before 1997, there is little hope that it will pick up after China resumes sovereignty. However, aside from economic experts, of whom there are many in Hong Kong, the territory will have to foster a new breed of people, hitherto unknown in the colony: politicians. British colonial officials will have to be gradually replaced by indigenous political leaders, and a new system of government will have to be created.

The Hong Kong government, aware of the need for change, issued a Green Paper in July 1984, titled "The Further Development of Representative Government in Hong Kong." The Green Paper proposed that the 47-member Legislative Council evolve in three stages into a body where at least some of the members are elected. However, for various reasons, it ruled out direct elections, proposing instead the setting up of an electoral college as well as elections by so-called functional groups. In the two months following publication of the Green Paper, there was extensive public response to its proposals. The principle of making the government more directly accountable to the people of Hong Kong by rooting its authority firmly in the community was widely hailed. Almost all sectors of the public recognized the need for reforms, though there were differences as to exactly what changes were needed, and the pace at which they were to be adopted. Some felt it was better to move slowly and cautiously down the untried road toward democracy, but others argued that, because Hong Kong only has a dozen years before it is to be an autonomous territory within the PRC, the pace needed to be quickened. A mass meeting was held in September 1984, at which dozens of organizations came out in support of direct elections, calling for at least a third of the legislature's members to be directly elected in 1988.

In late November 1984, the Hong Kong government made public its decision on the matter in a White Paper. The government moved up its timetable for shifting from an appointive to an elective system by about three years, so that what was planned for 1988 would come about in 1985. However, appointed members and civil servants would still be in the majority.

"If an element of continuity is to be maintained in the Legislative Council," the White Paper said, "it would be unwise to reduce appreciably or too hastily the number of appointed members at this stage, for their experience in the workings of the council should not be lost."

For the time being, at least, the government had decided not to take action on two major issues. The first was the proposal for direct elections. While "there was strong public support for the idea of direct elections," the White Paper said, there was "little support for such elections in the immediate future." However, the government said, a review will be held in 1987 to decide on the future mix of appointed and elected members, as well as the possibility of adopting direct elections.

The other major proposal for governmental reform that was set aside, at least for the time being, was the instituting of a ministerial system of government, under which government departments would be headed by "ministers" drawn from elected members of the legislature, as is done in Britain, rather than by civil servants.

The original White Paper had proposed that legislators might in the future select one of their own members to replace the governor in his role as president of the Legislative Council. The White Paper said that, on the whole, this suggestion was well received but that public opinion seemed to favor caution in making changes in the immediate future. Therefore, this reform, too, was temporarily shelved and is to be taken up in the review in 1987.

The White Paper did recognize one pressing need—the need for professional politicians. Up to now, appointed legislators had served without pay, usually taking time out from regular jobs to serve the community. But if the burden of running Hong Kong is to be shifted from the shoulders of British civil servants, then being a member of the legislature must become a full-time job. The government has decided that, beginning in 1985, legislators will receive a salary, though the level of pay remains to be determined.

Political coming-of-age

Preparing Hong Kong's people to run Hong Kong is a formidable task. To forestall disruption in 1997, a predominantly local administration will have to be in place well before then. Cooperation between Britain and China will be needed. For there to be a smooth transition, Britain's plans to reform the government system and China's drafting of the Basic Law must mesh.

In the meantime, another major change must take place. The largely apolitical inhabitants will have to learn to take an interest in their own governance. Political parties, or their equivalent, are likely to emerge. Several have already come into being in recent months, while more-established organizations may transform themselves into such political bodies. A climate will have to be created in which indigenous leaders may develop. This is easier said than done because, for well over 100 years, all political power resided with the British. Hong Kong's people, denied a significant role in the running of their own affairs, channeled their energies into other activities, the most popular of which was making money.

These future leaders will have to possess exceptional qualities. They will have to work for Hong Kong's interests while being sensitive to China's feelings about sovereignty and its modernization needs. People identified now as "pro-Chinese" or "pro-British" will have to put aside their differences and work together. They will also have to tread a thin line between left and right and avoid dividing and demoralizing the public.

Many people have spoken in terms of Hong Kong requiring a "Lee Kuan Yew" (Singapore's leader since 1959) to take over after 1997. However, the emergence of such a strong, independent-minded leader is unlikely since Hong Kong is not headed for independence. What is really needed is not one leader but a generation of leaders who can vigorously assert Hong Kong's autonomous status while never challenging China's sovereignty and the need for cooperation with Beijing.

District board elections

The first step toward this goal was taken in March 1985. On March 7, Hong Kong held its first territorywide elections, in which two thirds of the members of all District Boards were elected, with the remaining one third to be appointed by the government. Interest in the District Board elections was enhanced because members of District Boards would form an electoral college in September 1985 and, for the first time, elect 10 members of the Legislative Council.

On election day, almost half a million people—37.5 percent of all registered voters—cast their ballots at polling stations, an impressive turnout considering the lowly functions of District Boards. In the absence of political parties, the 501 candidates contesting the 237 seats generally ran as independents, though some political alliances were formed. Candidates were also fielded by the Civic Association and the Reform Club, two old, large civic bodies, as well as by some pressure groups and labor unions. A relatively small number of pro-Beijing and pro-Taiwan candidates also took part. The campaigns themselves were subdued, with emphasis put on service to Hong Kong and to the particular district.

The election threw up a host of new faces. Almost a fifth of the successful candidates were below the age of 30. Businessmen accounted for the largest single group. A sizable minority of people from the lower socioeconomic strata, such as factory workers, were also elected. The election itself may not have been a great exercise in democracy, but it was a valuable lesson for both the candidates and the electorate, many of whom are relatively unsophisticated. Some campaign workers, instead of emphasizing the platform of their candidate, handled the election like a horse race, telling people, for example, to vote for No. 3 "because it is a lucky number."

The September 1985 elections for the Legislative Council mark another, much greater, step. It is still too early to say for sure whether a reliable leadership structure will emerge. But the chances are fairly good.

The need for stability

Perhaps the most important thing for Hong Kong to keep in mind is the need not to rock the boat. Both Britain and China have made it clear that they are more interested in stability than in change. Democracy without prosperity will spell Hong Kong's demise, but the territory will be able to survive, and survive well, if there is prosperity without democracy.

In any event, the Joint Declaration calls for Britain to hand over government to China, not a local Hong Kong leadership, in 1997. Most people are agreed that such a transition should be smooth, so that July 1, 1997, will not be very different from June 30, 1997. If Britain and China can cooperate well in the next decade, it is possible to imagine that the past British-appointed governor of Hong Kong will also be the first Chinese-appointed chief executive of the Special Administrative Region.

Britain's political blueprint

The steps outlined by the British to prepare Hong Kong for representative government are extremely conservative. This is due in part to the innate conservatism of the Hong Kong government, which has a built-in distrust of democracy. In part, it is also due to fear of alarming China by moving too quickly. The Chinese have not commented on British plans for the political development of Hong Kong, ostensibly because of their undertaking to leave Britain in control until 1997. In reality, it is likely that China is keeping its own options open. If events move in a direction to its liking, China can retain whatever setup evolves. At the same time, China has the choice of repudiating a political structure built under British auspices. China, like Britain, will tolerate democracy in Hong Kong up to a point. But it wants to retain ultimate control.

The Taiwan factor

The cautious manner in which the Hong Kong government is moving reflects a fear—shared by the Chinese government and much of the Hong Kong public—that elections may polarize a community where the government has emphasized rule by consensus. There is also apprehension that people who have had no previous government experience may, in order to win votes, support greatly expanded social welfare programs that the government can ill afford, resulting in tax increases that will drive business away from Hong Kong. In addition, of course, there is fear that pro-Communist or pro-Taiwan people will dominate the legislature, to the detriment of Hong Kong.

China's fears of sabotage by pro-Taiwan elements appear real, if not necessarily well-founded. It is hard to see how it can be in Taiwan's interest to create unrest in Hong Kong. True, the fomenting of riots and other disturbances in post-1997 Hong Kong would bring the People's Liberation Army into action, and thus result in direct intervention by Beijing in Hong Kong's affairs. This would make Beijing look bad in the eyes of the world. But Taiwan's economy is so closely linked with that of Hong Kong that it would be a case of cutting off Taiwan's nose to spite China's face. There is, however, the danger that pro-Taiwan elements may take disruptive action without specific authorization from Taiwan, or perhaps with the authorization of only part of a factionalized leadership. The Taiwan issue shows the fragility of Hong Kong and the extent to which the territory is subject to external forces over which it has little if any influence.

China's leaders have made it clear that, while Taiwan would not be allowed to conduct "two China" activities in Hong Kong, Taiwanese organizations can continue to function. Mr. Deng has also said that the future Hong Kong government should include people from both the left and the right, but that the majority should be middle of the road.

Meeting a delegation of people from Hong Kong who went to Beijing to celebrate National Day, Mr. Deng assured them that China would not intervene in Hong Kong affairs or dictate to Hong Kong's leaders. He said: "The people of Hong Kong should close ranks and select good, qualified personnel to administer Hong Kong. This is your own business. What Beijing should do is only approve the persons you have selected and recommended." This sounds reassuring enough, but Mr. Deng is also reported to have said that if intervention is good for Hong Kong, there is no reason to fear it.

Drafting the Basic Law

Much depends on the Basic Law under which Hong Kong is to be governed. At this writing, it remains unclear how big a role Hong Kong's people will play in drafting this fundamental piece of legislation, which is to be adopted by China's legislature. While the Joint Declaration is primarily a statement of China's intentions, the Basic Law will provide the framework for all future Hong Kong legislation. It remains to be seen whether, in transforming principles into law, the rights of the people of Hong Kong and the existing system will be safeguarded.

For example, Chinese officials from Mr. Deng on down have said that "two China" activities will not be tolerated. If Beijing bans pro-Taiwan rallies (which can now be held if a police permit is obtained), prohibits the display of the Nationalist emblem (such as those on the aircraft of China Airlines, Taiwan's flag-carrier) and bars the use of such terms as "Republic of China" or "the President of Taiwan" from the press, people in Hong Kong will feel that their rights and freedoms are being eroded. Politicization of many of Hong Kong's long-standing practices can only inhibit, not enhance, the territory's ability to continue to prosper and to contribute to China's economic modernization.

Chinese leaders have also said repeatedly that future leaders of Hong Kong will have to be "patriotic." This constant harping on the need for "patriotism" can be damaging. Candidates running for election are likely to say things they feel China wants to hear, and campaign rhetoric could become increasingly China-oriented rather than Hong Kong-oriented. Xinhua and left-wing papers already openly label certain individuals as "patriotic," and the omission of such a label may be interpreted by the ultrasensitive Hong Kong public as meaning that other individuals are deemed by China to be "unpatriotic." A case in point occurred when Henry Fok, a businessman with close ties to the mainland, donated HK$100 million to China. He was described by both the left-wing press and Xinhua as "the well-known patriot Henry Fok."

For Hong Kong to remain prosperous, it must continue to play both a regional and international role in such areas as trade, finance, transportation and communications. In the post-1997 period, it is important for the rest of the world to perceive Hong Kong as an entity which, while under Chinese sovereignty, is different from the rest of China. However, there is a danger that the reverse may occur, and that Hong Kong's international standing may diminish. The Joint Declaration makes clear that some of the consular and other official missions in Hong Kong will have to be downgraded because they are from countries with which China has no diplomatic relations or that China does not recognize. Some of Hong Kong's most important trading partners fall into this category. Downgrading of their representative offices inevitably will result in a decline in Hong Kong's international standing and may make it more difficult for travel between Hong Kong and those places. This situation will be aggravated if Hong Kong will be unable to remain a member of some international bodies as a result of the change in government.

Such a development, coupled with a simultaneous politicization of the community, will greatly hamper Hong Kong's ability to continue to do business. China's promise of "no change for 50 years" will then appear hollow to many people.

This is not to say that Hong Kong's future is necessarily bleak. It is important to be aware of the potential pitfalls, so that they can be avoided. But, like so much that has to do with its future, the solutions to these problems are not in Hong Kong's hands.

In the period between now and 1997, China's influence in Hong Kong will be increasingly felt. Statements by Chinese leaders will be interpreted from every possible perspective. Although the Joint Liaison Group will be heavily involved in decisions that affect Hong Kong's future, its deliberations, like the Sino-British negotiations, are to be confidential. The Land Commission, another Sino-British body, may be called upon to make decisions that will affect the Hong Kong economy. Revenue from land has traditionally accounted for a substantial portion of the Hong Kong government's income, but now a ceiling has been placed on the amount of land the government can dispose of each year, and the government has to set aside half the revenue generated for use by the future Special Administrative Region. This loss in revenue has to be made up either by increasing taxes or cutting services. If such measures are not adequate, then the Hong Kong government may be forced to ask China for permission either to raise the ceiling on the amount of land to be made available each year or to dip into the funds of the Special Administrative Region. With a hold on the purse strings, China's influence in Hong Kong will become increasingly tangible. Even though the Joint Declaration specifies that responsibility for running Hong Kong will remain with Britain until 1997, China's shadow will loom increasingly large as time goes on.

香港

4

The Future:
View from Beijing

Back in 1979, Mr. Deng defined three major tasks for China in the
1980s: modernizing the economy, combating hegemonism (domination by the two superpowers) and reunifying the nation. Needless to
say, none of those tasks is likely to be completed within the decade. But
China has made significant progress on all three fronts. It has
revitalized its economy; it has forged an independent foreign policy,
improving its relationship with both the United States and the Soviet
Union, and it has negotiated an agreement with Britain for the return
of Hong Kong.

Actually, China could have asked Britain for Hong Kong at any
time in the last 20 years and not have received much of an argument.
Britain could not hope to hold on to Hong Kong militarily. Moreover,
the colony was dependent on Chinese goodwill for its survival because
the mainland provided Hong Kong with most of its drinking water and
food.

But until the 1980s China had no desire to take Hong Kong back.
China was preoccupied with its own internal problems and did not
want to deal with the Hong Kong issue until its hand was forced. The
decade-long Cultural Revolution tore the country apart and, in its
aftermath, the country's domestic problems appeared almost insurmountable.

China's hand was forced by Hong Kong residents and business people who wanted the uncertainty of 1997 removed. The British government in London, responding to Hong Kong pressure, officially sought China's views on the issue. With the benefit of hindsight, it appears that Hong Kong and Britain grossly miscalculated China's possible reaction. While Beijing may have been willing, as the Chinese saying goes, "to keep one eye open and the other eye closed" and to tolerate a colonial enclave that was financing China's modernization, it was politically impossible for any Chinese government to openly endorse a continuation of foreign rule over part of Chinese territory. The return of Hong Kong to China was a matter of principle not just to the Communists, but also to their Nationalist predecessors and the current government in Taiwan. So Beijing, once confronted by the problem of what to do about Hong Kong, had no choice but to call for the reversion of Hong Kong to China.

Quite ingeniously, Mr. Deng devised a formula under which he hoped to kill three birds with one stone—that of "one country, two systems." Applying this formula, China was able to negotiate the return of Hong Kong, hopefully preserve the territory as a moneymaking machine for China, and possibly create a model that might one day lure Taiwan back to "the embrace of the motherland."

The first goal has already been achieved. Now China is working to ensure the success of its second goal: the continued prosperity of Hong Kong. At the same time, it is intensifying its overtures to Taiwan.

Hong Kong is important to China's modernization efforts for many reasons. The one most often mentioned is as a foreign-exchange earner for China. But Hong Kong's usefulness goes far beyond that. Just as Western countries have long considered Hong Kong a window on China, so China considers Hong Kong its window on the outside world. From Hong Kong, China can expect to learn modern management methods, import Western technology and attract funds for investment. In the last few years, China has sent numerous study groups to Hong Kong, and Hong Kong's impact on China is already visible. Many foreign companies with offices in China prefer to bring in staff from Hong Kong rather than hire unskilled and unreliable personnel in China or bring in expensive expatriates from their own countries. Tour guides in the major tourist centers in China have had to learn Cantonese because of the big influx of free-spending Hong Kong visitors.

The economic argument for China to maintain Hong Kong as a capitalist enclave after 1997 is very strong, since the interests of China and Hong Kong coincide: if Hong Kong prospers, China will benefit, whereas if Hong Kong falls on hard times, it will only add to China's problems—an additional 5.5 million people to feed, most of whom can be expected to be strenuously opposed to absorption by the mainland.

It is true that, as China continues to open up to the outside world, the role of Hong Kong may diminish in a relative sense. But Hong Kong's role as a financial, trade and transshipment center is unlikely to be taken over by any mainland Chinese city. In China's attempt to catch up with the rest of the world, it will certainly not be in its interest to turn one of its principal stepping-stones into a stumbling block.

The political argument for keeping Hong Kong's status quo is likely to weigh even more heavily in the minds of Chinese leaders. Ever since 1949, the Nationalist government in Taiwan has been a thorn in Beijing's side, challenging its legitimacy and threatening to overthrow it. Aging Chinese leaders dearly wish to see a reunified China in their lifetimes, a wish shared by many Chinese in Taiwan and overseas.

With one eye on Taiwan, China has pledged that the capitalist system will be maintained in Hong Kong, that Beijing will not send officials to administer the territory, and that Hong Kong will be able to run its own economic affairs. Chinese officials have gone out of their way to show both to people in Hong Kong and to the international community at large that China fully intends to honor its commitments. Mr. Deng, on October 3, 1984, told visitors from Hong Kong who were in Beijing for the National Day celebrations:

> The policy of our party and our government toward the solution of the Hong Kong issue is to practice the idea of 'one country, two systems,' to allow Hong Kong people to administer Hong Kong, to send no personnel from the central authorities to Hong Kong, and not to interfere in the administrative affairs of Hong Kong. We will comply with the Sino-British joint agreement and time will confirm our readiness for this.

Mr. Deng staked the prestige of the Chinese government on its observance of the agreement. He said: "Since the Korean War, China has won a good reputation internationally. Even in the years of turmoil [the Cultural Revolution] the Chinese people meant what they said in international affairs. Acting in good faith is a tradition of our nation and also its strong point. This really indicates that ours is a great, proud and ancient country. A big nation should have its own dignity and its own principles to follow."

Open-door policy

China's policy toward Hong Kong is part and parcel of its open-door policy. Under this policy, trade has soared, foreigners have been invited to invest in China, four special economic zones have been established in southern China, and, in 1984, 14 coastal cities and Hainan Island were opened up to foreign investors. More recently, Chinese leaders have announced the opening up of vast regions along the coast, each comprising a number of cities, such as the Pearl River Delta area, the Yangtse River Delta area and the Shandong Peninsula. In addition, China has adopted many of the tools commonly associated with capitalism, giving emphasis to the role of the market, restricting the scope of central planning and granting much greater independence to managers of enterprises.

Statements by Chinese leaders have been unambiguous. Mr. Deng told a Japanese delegation in October 1984 that China would stay open to the outside world at least until the middle of the 21st century, and that by then it would be too late to change the nation's policy, since China would be so integrated into the world economy. The implication is that the open-door policy will remain forever.

The Deng succession

But these promises are being made by a man in his 80s. It is impossible to tell how much longer he can remain politically active. The big question is, what will happen to China after Mr. Deng goes?

The fact that this question is often asked indicates that China is not yet regarded as politically stable. This is true not because China is a Communist country but rather because it is an Asian society with a tradition of autocratic rule. Similar questions about political stability are frequently raised about, say, Taiwan after President Chiang Ching-kuo, or Singapore after Prime Minister Lee Kuan Yew, or the Philippines after President Ferdinand E. Marcos.

Mr. Deng's chosen successors are the 69-year-old party leader, Hu Yaobang, and the 65-year-old premier, Zhao Ziyang. However, even though they bear the titles, no one in China or abroad doubts that Mr. Deng, the chairman of the party's Central Advisory Commission, is really the one in charge. While he has theoretically "withdrawn to the second line," no major decision is made without his approval.

Mr. Deng has said that he hopes to retire at the age of 85. He appears to be in good health, and so it is quite possible that he may be able to continue running things for five more years. But what this means is that, when he finally steps down, his two handpicked successors will themselves be in their 70s, and the question of who will succeed them, as well as doubts about continuity of policies, will again become acute.

In some ways, China today is already a gerontocracy. The country's highest policymaking body, the Standing Committee of the Politburo, has six members: Deng is 80, Ye Jianying 87, Chen Yun 79, Li Xiannian 75, Hu Yaobang 69, and Zhao Ziyang, who, at 65, is the youngest.

The fact that Mr. Deng is still in charge implies that his two protégés are not quite ready to take over—they still require his prestige, influence and connections. If Mr. Deng should vanish from the scene tomorrow, it would certainly create a political vacuum. His protégés may require the political support of some other party elder—say Chen Yun, Li Xiannian, or Peng Zhen. All of these men are in their 70s or 80s, and there is a danger that China, like the Soviet Union in the last three years, will see a succession of old men.

There is at present very little overt opposition to Mr. Deng's policies—a situation very different from that in the late 1960s and early 1970s, when two factions were clearly identifiable.

This is not to say that everyone supports current policies to the same extent. In fact, recent statements by Chinese leaders and in the Chinese press have referred with increasing frequency to "some people," unnamed, who are always "afraid of capitalism," that is, they have reservations about China's opening to the West. The most likely successor to Mr. Deng as party elder, the economist Chen Yun, is known for his predilection for Soviet-style central planning. When the Soviet Union's first deputy premier, Ivan V. Arkhipov, visited China in late 1984, Mr. Chen was the most senior leader to meet him. At a time when China had just announced a greater role for the market, Mr. Chen chose to tell the Soviet visitor that what China and the Soviet Union had in common was a planned economy.

Recent events in China indicate that unhappiness over the ramifications of the open-door policy is widespread. In March 1985, the State Council issued a directive banning the holding of lotteries, a practice that was spreading uncontrollably in the mainland and that is very popular in Hong Kong. That same month a beauty contest in Canton, the first since the PRC was established, provoked great controversy. Articles in the official media indicated that economic crimes were rampant, with many cadres making use of their authority to engage in illegal transactions. Mr. Deng himself, at a conference on scientific work, acknowledged that the fear that China will turn capitalist is "not entirely groundless." He asserted that the open-door policy was aimed at developing socialism, not capitalism.

The military factor

Though there are no identifiable opposition leaders, this does not mean that they do not exist. As long as Mr. Deng is so firmly in charge, it would be foolhardy for anyone to oppose him openly. The military, in particular, is regarded as a hotbed of conservatism. The fact that Mr. Deng has retained the chairmanship of both the party and state military commissions which makes him commander in chief of the armed forces tends to confirm that the military is a force that only Mr. Deng can control. No one else has sufficient prestige to keep the military in check.

In the current campaign to reform the economy, the military is the target of a concerted drive. At a forum of the Central Military Commission, according to an authoritative article in the *People's Daily,* Mr. Deng stressed that "the work of the armed forces must be subordinate to the great affairs of national construction." This is diametrically opposed to the Maoist slogan of "putting politics in command" of all work.

Although there are no visible opponents of Deng's policies, there is a certain amount of lingering opposition in the minds of many people, from the very top of the leadership down to the man in the street. People in China have been steeped in anticapitalist ideology for decades. So-called ultraleft attitudes and prejudices are everywhere; they oppose such recent trends as women wearing makeup and perming their hair, not to mention the privileges enjoyed by foreigners in China.

In 1979, the Chinese produced a film marking 30 years of Communist rule; it showed Chinese laborers in the "bad old days" working and living under primitive conditions, while well-fed foreigners lounged on deck chairs, living off the Chinese people they were exploiting. The author could not help feeling that things had not changed that much, at least on the surface. Foreigners in China were still living much better than Chinese, and a similar film could be made today, contrasting the privileged lives of foreigners in Beijing with the lot of the Chinese masses. Ironically, however, the current situation was created by the Chinese themselves. The policy of isolating foreigners from Chinese aggravates the situation by inculcating suspicion of foreigners in the minds of ordinary people. This may well fuel another outbreak of xenophobia. But time may alleviate the problem as the general standard of living rises and as ordinary Chinese have access to the better things in life. The Chinese are showing signs of tackling the problem through such measures as opening up restaurants in previously "foreigners only" hotels to local people.

Chinese officials have a standard response when doubts are voiced as to whether a new generation of leaders would change current policies: as long as the policies benefit the Chinese people, no one will be able to change them. However, events in the last few decades have shown that the Communist party was able to institute many policies that were extremely unpopular: movements such as the antirightist campaign (which squelched the Hundred Flowers Movement, characterized by free speech and criticism of the Chinese Communist party), the Great Leap Forward, which resulted in a famine that led to the death of millions of people, and then the Cultural Revolution. Yet the government and party were in no danger of being overthrown.

In fact, the Communist party is now patting itself on the back and saying that it was able to recognize its own mistakes and to correct them. That, however, does not mean that the party will not make new mistakes in the future. And if that should happen, the party may become more unpopular. That does not necessarily mean it will not be able to continue to rule.

Opposition to open door

From reading the Chinese press, it appears that there are two main, though related, objections to the open-door policy. One is social: It leads to corruption, degeneration of morals, crime, etc. The other is ideological: The party's revolutionary ideals are being betrayed and the traditional archenemy, capitalism, is being restored.

Not all opposition to current policies stems from ideology. Very real questions of personal interest are often involved. Large numbers of ordinary people have been harmed by the reforms. Party cadres, for instance, see their authority eroding and themselves shunted aside. The party committee secretary of a factory, whose preeminence used to be unquestioned, is now listed in fifth place, after the factory director, chief engineer, chief economist and chief accountant. In the countryside, party cadres who used to wield great power now find themselves with very little to do, as peasants are producing and selling directly to the market.

Most peasants, it seems clear, are benefiting from the new policy. One side effect is that the military is finding it harder to gain recruits, for able-bodied peasants prefer to stay with their family and increase its earning power. Even men actually serving in the armed forces frequently get telegrams from home at harvesttime to return to help with the work on the pretext that there is an illness in the family.

Even among the peasantry, there are some who are not benefiting from the reforms. People who live in resource-poor areas, no matter how hard they work, may not be able to prosper. And families with few able-bodied workers cannot take advantage of the maxim "more pay for more work." They may prefer the old system under which they were able to share in the collective's income, regardless of their contribution.

The increasing wealth of the peasantry has bred resentment among city workers. Employees of government departments compare their lot unhappily with those of factory workers, who can earn bonuses, and peasants, who can be in business for themselves. Office staff remain on fixed salaries and feel left out of the general rush to get rich. The widening gap between rich and poor has led several Chinese leaders to call on propaganda workers not to play up the "10,000-yuan families," who are rich by Chinese standards, apparently because it generated envy rather than spurred others on to work harder.

Chinese leaders have responded to the charge that the open-door policy is breeding unhealthy tendencies by cracking down periodically on crime and by enforcing party discipline. Capital punishment is frequently invoked for offenses ranging from murder to rape to robbery. In addition, young hoodlums are sent off to be "reformed through labor." At the same time, the leadership has sought to draw a distinction between natural human desires for a higher standard of living, characterized, for example, by more-stylish clothes, and manifestations of bourgeois tendencies. Recently, some people have even suggested that the Chinese word for the proletariat—*wu-chan-jie-ji,* or "propertyless class"—is inappropriate, since the party's goal is for everyone to become wealthy.

Doubtless, raising the standard of living is a popular goal. But the way this is being done must raise questions in the minds of many people about its ideological correctness. Ideology as a force may be waning, but it is still strong. At present, realism and pragmatism are the guiding lights, and ideology is being reduced to a justification of policies rather than treated as a guide in the formulation of policies.

Communist party chairman Mao wrote a letter to his wife Jiang Qing in which he said that, after his death, rightists would come to power. However, he said, eventually the left will be able to seize power again by overthrowing the right. Some people in China no doubt feel that the first part of this prediction has come true. How many are waiting for the second half to be fulfilled?

Assuring continuity

To forestall any such occurrence, Chinese officials are taking steps to weed out potential opponents who may be lying low, biding their time. Chinese leaders are hard at work fostering a new generation of like-minded people who will see that China continues on its present course even after the older generation passes from the scene. In the selection of successors, the Chinese have made it clear that "three kinds of people" will never be allowed to assume leadership positions at any level. These are defined as followers of Lin Biao and the Gang of'Four who rose to power in the Cultural Revolution, people who engaged in factionalism, and those who were involved in beating, smashing and looting during the Cultural Revolution. The current party rectification is aimed at weeding out these people. But this, too, has an inherent danger. It may create an underclass, possibly of millions of people, who feel that their only hope is the overthrow of the current leadership and the repudiation of its policies.

Mr. Deng was quoted in the authoritative Beijing magazine *Liaowang* as saying in 1981 that the succession problem is "a problem determining our fate." Mr. Deng added: "If it is not solved in three to five years, then there is likely to be chaos." His words reflect a sense of urgency. Much has been done in the last few years to solve this problem, but the process is not yet over. The party itself has taken the lead, rejuvenating the Central Committee. The 1982 elections to the Central Committee saw 211 new members admitted to the 348-member committee, an overwhelming majority. The day-to-day running of party affairs has been put in the hands of people in their 40s and 50s, such as Hu Qili, the 56-year-old former mayor of Tianjin. At the provincial level, the average age of leaders has dropped by six or seven years. Action to promote younger and better-educated people has also been taken at other levels as well as in the army, schools and businesses. Much emphasis is being placed on the importance of academic qualifications.

Chen Yun, another veteran party leader, has also addressed this important problem. He said: "We must train thousands upon thousands of middle-aged and young cadres; and let middle-aged and young cadres combining ability and political integrity train in leadership posts at various levels, and form a powerful reserve force for party and government work at various levels." As a result of this suggestion, *Liaowang* said, reserve forces are being established at all levels. "About 1,000 fine middle-aged and young cadres are being recommended as reserve forces for chief leaders at provincial and ministerial levels," the magazine reported. "More than 20,000 people are being recommended as reserve forces at the prefectural and bureau levels. Nearly 100,000 people are being recommended for reserve forces for leaders at the county level."

These steps have been taken to ensure continuity of policies when the present generation of leaders vanishes from the scene. They are very encouraging in that they seek to place capable, enlightened people in key positions across the country and throughout the bureaucracy. Such people tend to be pragmatic-minded technocrats. With China in their hands, the likelihood that ideological purists will succeed in bringing about a reversal of policies will recede with the years.

China's current leaders appear to have taken the offensive in explaining the ideological consistency of the new policies. Reversing the stance they took in the 1960s, when they accused the Russians of being "revisionists," China's leaders now say socialism must be adapted to suit each country's own characteristics. German Socialist Friedrich Engels is quoted as having said: "In my opinion, the so-called 'socialist society' is not something immutable but, like all other social systems, should be regarded as something changeable and reformable."

While Marxism embodies universal truths, Chinese leaders say, these have to be integrated with concrete realities, so that China can blaze its own path and build socialism with Chinese characteristics.

"Marxism does not bind people hand and foot," the ideological journal *Red Flag* said. "As long as our structural reform is conducive to building socialism with Chinese characteristics, to making our country prosperous and strong, and to making our people rich and happy, it conforms with Marxism."

The authoritative theoretical organ of the Communist party also argued that though China is learning advanced management methods from capitalist countries, those methods in themselves do not have class characteristics. "Their use will never lead to capitalism," *Red Flag* declared.

This argument harks back to the late 19th century, when some Chinese intellectuals called for making use of foreign technology while preserving China's essence. Chairman Mao, too, continued this line of reasoning, in his famous slogan, "Let the past serve the present, make foreign things serve China." The vehemence with which the case is being argued suggests that there are critics who find the argument unconvincing.

Even if there is no about-face in Chinese ideology, many people in Hong Kong are fearful that China will intervene, not necessarily for ideological reasons but simply because Communists have a record of being reluctant to delegate power.

Chinese intervention may also result because of developments in Hong Kong. If the Hong Kong government, in its dealings with Taiwan or foreign countries, takes actions that Beijing considers to be incompatible with China's sovereignty or basic Chinese policies, Beijing may feel compelled to step in. It is possible that intervention may be triggered by some politically insignificant event.

The exact relationship between Hong Kong and Beijing has not been spelled out, and this is one area that the Basic Law will have to tackle. Also needed are established channels of communication between Hong Kong and Beijing as well as between Hong Kong and Guangdong provincial authorities. Hong Kong will have to deal with the latter on such matters as provision of water and repatriation of illegal immigrants.

Revolution or evolution?

To the dialectically minded Chinese, nothing is static. Change is inevitable. But this does not mean that the pendulum must swing back to the radical leftism of the Cultural Revolution. Change can also take the form of evolution. And China today is clearly evolving. Just what "socialism with Chinese characteristics" will turn out to be like is still uncertain. But judging from the direction in which things are moving now, it will be quite different from the kind of socialism that had been practiced previously. It is likely to have much more in common with capitalist societies, such as that in Hong Kong.

Such a China is less likely to find Hong Kong an embarrassment, and there may be less political pressure on Beijing to intervene in Hong Kong's affairs. But if there are new power struggles and reversals of policies in China, Hong Kong will be in for rough times. Many people in the territory will trim their sails, doing and saying things that they think Beijing wants to see and hear. In the meantime, there may be an exodus of the very people Hong Kong needs most: its entrepreneurs, bankers, lawyers, accountants, doctors and architects, people who play an indispensable role in keeping an economy going.

If China does intervene, the effect will be proportionate to the amount of interference. There may be a flight of foreign and domestic capital, a disincentive to work, decline in productivity and a gradual erosion of individual rights as people fear to exercise them.

The next 12 to 13 years will provide many clues as to whether the Chinese government is likely to intervene in the day-to-day administration of Hong Kong. A new generation of Chinese leaders may well be in place long before 1997. People in Hong Kong are likely to have time to appraise the abilities and intentions of the new Chinese leadership well before the territory reverts to Chinese sovereignty. So much is at stake that all eyes in Hong Kong will be on developments in China for the next dozen years. Similarly, Hong Kong plays such a crucial role as the financial and communications hub of Southeast Asia that its neighbors will be watching the way Hong Kong develops with keen interest and concern.

香港

5

Conclusion

Hong Kong is the hub of communications in the Pacific and the financial center of Asia, and it operates the world's third-largest containerport. Maintenance of Hong Kong's prosperity and stability has implications that extend well beyond the territory. Any setbacks to Hong Kong, or any increases in its prosperity, will have repercussions regionally and globally.

The widespread interest in the Sino-British negotiations illustrates the concern felt in many capitals over the colony's future, and the openly voiced support for the agreement, with its detailed provisions for the continuation of the social and economic status quo, underlines a sense of general relief.

Immediately after the initialing of the agreement, the Chinese government acted to inform the whole world of its intentions toward Hong Kong. Foreign Minister Wu Xueqian, in his address to the UN the day after the Joint Declaration was initialed, explained to that international body China's policies toward Hong Kong.

The reaction was very positive. The secretary-general of the UN, Javier Pérez de Cuéllar, offered his congratulations to China and Britain for successfully resolving "a very delicate and complex issue."

The U.S. secretary of state, George P. Shultz, also welcomed the agreement, pledging American cooperation. In a message to Foreign Minister Wu, Mr. Shultz said: "The United States will provide any assistance it can, in close cooperation with the United Kingdom and the PRC, to maintain Hong Kong's appropriate participation in international bodies." Such an expression of support was most encouraging to Hong Kong, since the United States is the territory's largest market by far, accounting for over one third of Hong Kong's exports.

Support for the agreement also came from the European Economic Community (EEC), whose members are among Hong Kong's main trading partners, especially as importers of Hong Kong-made clothing and textiles, the colony's major exports. "This is an impressive achievement which augurs well for the future of Hong Kong as a prosperous and stable community," a statement issued by the foreign ministers of the EEC's 10 member states said.

Japan, which accounts for a large portion of foreign investment in Hong Kong, has also voiced official support for the Sino-British Joint Declaration. Other messages of support came from such disparate nations as Pakistan, Singapore, Thailand, Portugal and even North Korea. The Soviet Union reported the accord without comment.

Taiwan condemns accord

Virtually the only dissenting note in this chorus of congratulations came from Taiwan. On the day the agreement was initialed, Premier Yu Kuo-hwa issued a statement in which he accused the British government of "pushing 5.5 million people under Communist totalitarian enslavement, creating disgrace in human history." Taiwan's foreign minister Chu Fu-sung condemned the Joint Declaration as "a phony scheme as well as a political intrigue" and said the "one country, two systems" slogan was designed to apply political pressure on, and to isolate, Taiwan.

The Nationalists are now confronted with a dilemma. The official policy is to have no contact with the Chinese Communists. What is Taiwan to do when Hong Kong formally becomes part of the PRC? An article in the English-language *China Post* in Taipei, Taiwan's capital, illustrates the dimensions of the problem from Taiwan's point of view:

> Any type of communication between the Kuomintang [Nationalist party]-ruled Taiwan and Hong Kong under the Chinese Communist flag will be illegal after 1997 since the government prohibits direct exchange of transportation, mailing and trade with any part of Red China. The ban was set by authorities here for fear of being infiltrated by the Chinese Communists.
>
> To sever the country's connection with Hong Kong, however, will be very difficult because Taiwan relies on the bustling port as an entrepôt and an important base of its communications with foreign countries.
>
> According to official statistics offered by the Hong Kong government,

transit trade volume between Hong Kong and Taiwan reached HK$2.4
billion (U.S.$307.7 million) in the first half of this year. During that
period, Taiwan was Hong Kong's fourth largest exporter and the fifth
largest importer of Hong Kong-made products or transit goods from the
colony.

Flights between Taipei and Hong Kong are one of the most lucrative
routes in the world and are currently flown by 18 international airlines.
There are a total of 129 flights being operated between the two cities
every week.

The Republic of China national flag carrier, China Airlines, runs
32 regular flights to Hong Kong, of which 16 continue to other Asian
cities, including Bangkok, Singapore and Kuala Lumpur. A large part
of the island's information exchange abroad, including satellite and
telephone communications, also go through the free port.

Taiwan would hurt itself badly and increase its isolation if it were to
cut off ties with Hong Kong. But retention of such ties after 1997
would require greater flexibility than the Nationalist government has
demonstrated so far. It would be to the benefit of all three parties—
Taiwan, Hong Kong and China—for the ties to continue. In this
respect, Beijing is in a position to influence Taiwan's actions, since it
can render the atmosphere in Hong Kong totally uncongenial to
Taiwan or adopt tactics that will help Taiwan save face while
abandoning its rigid posture of having no dealings at all with any
portion of the PRC.

From China's point of view, therefore, Hong Kong can be seen as
bait to lure the Taiwan fish. If, after 1997, China violates its pledge not
to intervene in Hong Kong's internal affairs, this will doubtless
strengthen Taiwan's distrust of the Communists, and probably destroy
whatever chance there is for a dialogue that could lead to peaceful
reunification. If, on the other hand, China scrupulously honors its
pledge to Hong Kong and the world and the territory continues to
thrive, then Beijing will be able to point to Hong Kong as a model and
seek to persuade Taiwan that it does not stand to lose anything by an
accommodation with China.

ASEAN's view

For historical and political reasons, the accord on Hong Kong was
received with less enthusiasm in some Southeast Asian countries than
in the West. Suspicion of the Chinese Communists is still widespread
in such countries as Indonesia, Malaysia and Singapore. China has in
the past supported insurgent movements in those countries and, even
after establishing diplomatic relations with some countries, such as
Malaysia, insisted on continuing to give moral if not material support
to the rebels. The problem is compounded in that many of the rebels
are ethnic Chinese.

Indonesia, the largest country within the six-member Association of Southeast Asian Nations (ASEAN), suspended diplomatic relations with China formally in 1967, when it suspected that Beijing was the mastermind behind a pro-Communist coup attempt. Singapore, whose population consists largely of ethnic Chinese, has declined to establish diplomatic relations with China. One reason is that it does not want to subject its citizens to conflicting loyalties: loyalty to Singapore and loyalty to their ancestral homeland. Another reason is that Singapore does not want to be seen as a stalking horse for China in a region where racial tensions run high and both the Chinese government and ethnic Chinese are viewed with suspicion. For this reason, though Singapore has a trade office in Beijing, it has declared that it is in no hurry to recognize the Communist government there, and prefers to be the last member of ASEAN to take such action.

Southeast Asian countries have always viewed British-ruled Hong Kong as part of the non-Communist fraternity. Malaysia and Singapore also share with Hong Kong a common British heritage. With Hong Kong coming under Chinese sovereignty, some of the governments of the region will have to reassess their relationship with the territory. National security interests are involved. Some governments, for example, to safeguard the security of their communications, will no longer route them through Hong Kong.

If Southeast Asian countries do not believe that China will honor its Hong Kong pledges, they may restrict travel by their nationals to the territory and make it difficult for holders of Hong Kong travel documents to obtain visas. At present, most members of ASEAN do not allow their nationals to travel freely to the PRC, but they do permit such travel to Hong Kong. If these countries do not perceive Hong Kong as a genuinely separate entity after 1997, they may restrict travel by their nationals to Hong Kong and curtail visitors from the territory.

Such a development would affect not only Hong Kong but also China. Now, many ethnic Chinese from those countries are able to fly to Hong Kong, then slip unobtrusively into China to visit friends and relatives. If this channel is blocked, Beijing may find itself cutoff from many Southeast Asian Chinese.

The Chinese authorities are aware of this situation. They feel that overseas Chinese have an important role to play both in the nation's economic development and in Beijing's reunification efforts. This should give China additional incentive to preserve Hong Kong as an entity that is clearly different from the rest of the country.

In terms of trade, the ASEAN countries are much less important to Hong Kong than the major markets in North America and Western Europe. But, while the volume is small, it is not insignificant. Hong

Kong's imports from ASEAN account for 3 to 4 percent of that regional grouping's total exports, while the territory's exports account for only 1 to 2 percent of ASEAN's imports.

Because of uncertainty over the future of Hong Kong, there has been a certain amount of capital flight, as well as a small but significant "brain drain." The countries of Southeast Asia, on the whole, do not wish to accept large numbers of Hong Kong Chinese. But they are interested in taking advantage of Hong Kong's problems, primarily by attracting Hong Kong capital. From Hong Kong's viewpoint, the most desirable places for investment and possible settlement are such countries as the United States, Canada and Australia. But Hong Kong's Asian neighbors, including Singapore, Taiwan, Thailand and the Philippines, have also taken steps to try to attract Hong Kong entrepreneurs and their money. Singapore, being a predominantly Chinese society, is also interested in attracting highly skilled Hong Kong professionals and in possibly supplanting Hong Kong as Asia's banking center.

Although Hong Kong perhaps is not irreplaceable as a center for doing business in Asia, its efficiency, its infrastructure and its English-speaking professionals and secretaries are major assets. Tokyo is a more expensive city in which to operate, and the use of English is much less widespread than in Hong Kong. Other Asian countries are also hampered by too many restrictive regulations, such as currency controls, or by rampant corruption.

All in all, Hong Kong has been and remains an extremely desirable place to do business from the point of view of the Western businessman. Reaction by members of the foreign business community so far has reflected a sense of confidence that they can continue to work in Hong Kong. For example, Lawrence J. Toal, senior vice president of the Hong Kong branch of Chase Manhattan Bank, has been quoted as saying that the agreement, which is better than American businessmen in Hong Kong had expected, has dispelled anxiety and uncertainty about Hong Kong's future.

Future international role in question

One of Hong Kong's major concerns has been whether, after the transfer of government authority to China in 1997, the territory will be able to continue to participate in international organizations and be a party to international agreements.

Well over 400 international agreements are involved, including about 300 international treaties and accords and 160 bilateral agreements entered into by Britain that apply to Hong Kong. At present, the Hong Kong government's legal experts are in the process of examining each of them with a view to deciding how best its value can be preserved after Hong Kong reverts to China in 1997. Maintaining Hong Kong's separate international identity is crucial if the territory is to continue to function.

The problem is serious but not necessarily insurmountable. Hong Kong, for example, is able to participate in GATT, the most important of these accords. China is not a member and so, if Hong Kong's ties with Britain are severed today, the territory's link with GATT would be in jeopardy. But if China joins the world trade agreement before 1997, it can take over the role that Britain has played and provide for Hong Kong's continued participation.

China is already a member of GATT's textile committee, and has been invited to take part in all meetings of the GATT council. Chinese officials have indicated that China is giving active consideration to joining GATT, and that it would be possible for a Hong Kong representative to join the Chinese delegation. If this happens, Hong Kong will merely have to switch sponsors in 1997. However, Hong Kong's role in certain international activities may be broken off in 1997 because China is not a participant. Membership in British Commonwealth organizations and agreements is a case in point, though even there it is possible that an observer status may be preserved for Hong Kong.

Links with such organizations as GATT, the Multifiber Arrangement, the International Monetary Fund and the Asian Development Bank constitute Hong Kong's economic lifeline and must be maintained. Both China and Britain recognize this. So far, the signs are encouraging that Hong Kong will be able to make a transition from a British Crown Colony to a Chinese Special Administrative Region with a minimum of economic disruption.

Lawyers reserve judgment

While the business community as a whole has been voicing optimism, neither of Hong Kong's two professional legal associations, the Bar Association and the Law Society, has taken an official position on the draft agreement. It is perhaps not surprising that lawyers would withhold their approval. The entire draft agreement depends on one article of the Chinese constitution for its legality, Article 31, which gives the state the right to establish Special Administrative Regions. However, Article 31 does not say that the rest of the Chinese constitution will not apply to Special Administrative Regions, and nowhere in the constitution does it say that people who live in these regions need not abide by other articles in the constitution.

To some people, therefore, the legality of Special Administrative

Regions, and indeed the validity of Article 31, may be open to challenge.

People who believe that Hong Kong can function successfully as a Special Administrative Region apparently assume that there is no conflict between the Joint Declaration and the constitution. Such an assumption appears unwarranted. The Joint Declaration is clearly in violation of both the spirit and the letter of much of the constitution. The preamble of the constitution calls that document "the fundamental law of the state" and says that "the people of all nationalities, all state organs, the armed forces, all political parties and public organizations, and all enterprises and undertakings in the country must take the constitution as the basic norm of conduct, and they have the duty to uphold the dignity of the constitution and ensure its implementation."

The constitution spells out the socialist nature of China in its first article. "The PRC is a socialist state under the people's democratic dictatorship led by the working class and based on the alliance of workers and peasants," it says. "The socialist system is the basic system of the PRC. Sabotage of the socialist system by any organization or individual is prohibited."

Just what socialism means is explained in Article 6. "The basis of the socialist economic system of the PRC is socialist public ownership of the means of production, namely, ownership by the whole people and collective ownership by the working people," it says. "The system of socialist public ownership supersedes the system of exploitation of man by man." The system of "exploitation of man by man" is part of the Communist definition of capitalism.

In view of these and other articles, the significance of Article 31 may be seen in a very different light. If the Chinese government permits Hong Kong a separate legal system, it would appear to be in violation of Article 33, which says that "all citizens of the PRC are equal before the law." If Chinese citizens in Hong Kong are governed under different laws, then treatment clearly is not equal. Hong Kong, for instance, has effectively eliminated capital punishment, while the death penalty is relatively common in China.

If the Chinese government permits capitalism to be practiced in Hong Kong, the government itself may be judged to be in violation of the constitution. This is because Article 24 says "the state . . . combats capitalist, feudal and other decadent ideas." If the state abdicates its responsibility to combat capitalism in one part of China, namely Hong Kong, it would appear to be guilty of dereliction of duty.

Yet the Basic Law, which is a local law applicable only to the Special Administrative Region of Hong Kong, is supposed to stipulate that "the socialist system and the socialist policies shall not be practiced in the Hong Kong Special Administrative Region and that Hong

Kong's previous capitalist system and lifestyle shall remain unchanged for 50 years."

Constitutional flexibility

Perhaps what this serves to illustrate is that in China laws and constitutions do not count for much. After all, the same people responsible for drafting the constitution were also responsible for working out the agreement with Britain. In China, policy is still more important than law, and policies are often formulated by individual leaders who rely on their personal influence rather than the office they hold to carry the day. In the long run, whether Hong Kong will prosper depends not so much on what laws and regulations are written down on paper as on how China perceives its own interests. For Hong Kong to survive more or less in its present form, it is more important that the territory continue to meet China's needs than for the Joint Declaration or Basic Law to conform with the constitution. But, if China is mindful of the disquiet on the part of Hong Kong's people and of foreigners who place greater weight on laws and constitutions than does China, it may find it advisable to remove the constitutional ambiguities that exist.

However, the publicity China has given to the agreement, both domestically and internationally, certainly indicates a willingness to abide by its terms. Moreover, for China, much more is at stake than the prosperity of Hong Kong. China has put its national reputation on the line. The "four modernizations" program (simultaneous advances in agriculture, industry, science and technology, and defense) can be greatly facilitated if Hong Kong plays its proper role.

Failure to honor the agreement on China's part would undoubtedly lead to another crisis in Hong Kong, even more severe than that of September 1983. It would cripple Hong Kong, and would also cause a severe decline in China's credibility, not only with Britain but with the rest of the world. China's own major trading partners—the United States, Japan and Western Europe—all have a stake in Hong Kong's continued success. Beijing will certainly not lightly embark upon any course that will damage its carefully nurtured relations with the major countries of the non-Communist world. Not honoring the Hong Kong agreement will be a sure way of deterring foreign investors from putting their money in China itself.

China has another important stake in maintaining Hong Kong's stability and prosperity: Taiwan. Chinese leaders have said since the Joint Declaration was initialed that the formula of "one country, two systems" was applicable to Taiwan as well. China is offering Taiwan the status of a Special Administrative Region too, so Taiwan will be closely watching Beijing's attitude toward Hong Kong. Even if Taiwan and Beijing were to discuss a different form of association, such as a

federation, the degree of Taiwan's confidence in Beijing's word would
be greatly affected by China's actions in Hong Kong.

Closer to home, China is also aware that its Asian neighbors view
Hong Kong as a test of whether China has really abandoned radical
political objectives for economic development. Open intervention by
Beijing in Hong Kong's affairs would be certain to backfire, setting
back years of diplomatic efforts.

While China's nonintervention in Hong Kong affairs after 1997 is
an essential ingredient for the territory's prosperity and stability, the
situation between now and 1997 is different. In the transition period, it
is necessary for China to cooperate with Britain. There are many areas
that require such cooperation. Obtaining international recognition of
Hong Kong's special status is one. Working out a future government
structure for Hong Kong is another. China will also need to devise a
Basic Law acceptable to Hong Kong. All the preparatory work for
Hong Kong to function effectively as a Special Administrative Region
will have to be completed before 1997. After that date, China will have
to limit itself to the twin spheres of defense and foreign policy, leaving
the administration of Hong Kong to local residents.

All this presupposes Britain's cooperation in the years leading up to
1997. Britain will have to consult China on its plans for the development of a new government structure. The two countries will presumably be working in harmony through their representatives on the Joint
Liaison Group and the Land Commission. Since a precipitate, overnight change on July 1, 1997, would certainly be harmful, Britain will
have to accept a reduced role in the running of Hong Kong as the
deadline approaches. Care will have to be exercised during the
transition period to see to it that the British government is not rendered
so impotent that the British will find the situation untenable and hasten
their own departure. That Britain will continue to administer Hong
Kong until 1997 is an important ingredient of the agreement; a British
pullout before that time would deal a severe blow to the birth of the
Special Administrative Region.

Rx for Hong Kong: Caution

Hong Kong residents will need to exercise care not to provoke
China, consciously or otherwise. The best way for Hong Kong to
forestall Chinese intervention is to make sure that there is no possible
excuse for such action by keeping its own house in order and seeing to it
that there are no serious outbreaks of civil commotion. While
continuing to trade and do other business with Taiwan, Hong Kong
must not tilt toward Taiwan politically. The government will have to
take care not to encourage an independence movement. It will also have

a responsibility to see to it that China's enemies are not able to use Hong Kong as a springboard for activities that are inimical to Chinese interests, such as intelligence-gathering.

Above all, Hong Kong will have to do its best to maintain its own economic prosperity. China is much more likely to keep its hands off a prosperous Hong Kong that is contributing to China's development than a Hong Kong that has fallen victim to an economic slump. If Hong Kong's exports should decline sharply, it would lose its ability to pay for large-scale imports from China, and hence its value to China would diminish. This could lead China to question the wisdom of maintaining Hong Kong as a capitalist enclave. The continued prosperity of Hong Kong is the best guarantee of China's nonintervention.

Granted a political framework in which Hong Kong's people can have confidence, the territory's continued economic prosperity is more than likely. Hong Kong enjoys certain advantages, such as its geographical location, the time zone in which it is situated and its natural harbor, which coupled with a hard-working labor force, an efficient bureaucracy, talented entrepreneurs and reliable health, educational, housing and police services have accounted to a large extent for the territory's past prosperity. If all these elements remain in the years leading up to and beyond 1997, the chances of maintaining prosperity are good. The one factor that most people consider to be the joker in the deck is China's attitude. It will be important for Hong Kong to understand China better, just as it is essential for China to understand Hong Kong and how it works. The machinery has worked well and any tinkering by China is likely to be counterproductive.

If China's current open-door policy continues, its understanding of Hong Kong is also likely to be enhanced. The more the open cities and the special economic zones, such as Shenzhen, develop, the more they will resemble Hong Kong. And if the leaders in Beijing can accept such a transformation in Shenzhen and other parts of Guangdong province, they are more likely to be accepting and understanding of Hong Kong. But even if Beijing should retrench and narrow the scope of the open-door policy in future years, it is much more likely to move against economic zones on the mainland than it is to take any action against Hong Kong, since it is relatively easy for China to seal itself off from what it may deem to be the undesirable influence of Hong Kong.

The Joint Declaration signed by Britain and China is by no means the last word on the subject of Hong Kong's future. It is a good first step, given that the British administration was coming to an end. Much more remains to be done. The agreement is fragile and needs careful nurturing by all parties concerned, China, Britain and the people of Hong Kong, in the years leading up to and beyond 1997. ∎

Chronology

1842	Treaty of Nanking; Hong Kong Island ceded to Britain in perpetuity
1860	Convention of Peking; southern Kowloon Peninsula and Stonecutters Island ceded to Britain in perpetuity
1898	Convention of Peking; New Territories leased to Britain for 99 years
1941–45	Japanese occupation of Hong Kong
1949	People's Republic of China established
1958–60	Great Leap Forward
1965	Cultural Revolution begins
1976	Mao Zedong dies; Cultural Revolution ends
1979	Sir Murray MacLehose, governor of Hong Kong, raises in Beijing the question of Hong Kong's future, specifically land leases expiring in 1997
September 1982	Margaret Thatcher and Deng Xiaoping open diplomatic channels for the "first phase" of negotiations
Spring 1983	Thatcher's private messages to Premier Zhao Ziyang suggest sovereignty issue be set aside; break deadlock in negotiations
July 12, 1983	"Second phase" of negotiations begins; first of 22 rounds of talks
October 1983	Beijing confirms September 1984 as deadline for an agreement to be reached, or else China will proceed with its own plans for Hong Kong
Fall 1983	China gives guarantee that Hong Kong's existing system will remain unchanged for 50 years after 1997
April 20, 1984	Sir Geoffrey Howe, Secretary of State for Foreign and Commonwealth Affairs, states that British administration will end in Hong Kong after 1997
May 25, 1984	Deng Xiaoping states that People's Liberation Army troops will be stationed in Hong Kong after 1997
August 1, 1984	Both sides agree to establish a Sino-British Joint Liaison Group to oversee the agreement until the year 2000
September 26, 1984	Joint Declaration initialed by British Ambassador Sir Richard Evans and Deputy Foreign Minister Zhou Nan
December 19, 1984	Thatcher and Zhao formally sign the Sino-British Joint Declaration (and three annexes)
May 27, 1985	Agreement comes into effect with exchange of instruments of ratification of Joint Declaration in Beijing
June 30, 1997	Britain's 99-year lease on the New Territories expires

APPENDIX

JOINT DECLARATION
OF THE GOVERNMENT OF THE UNITED KINGDOM OF
GREAT BRITAIN AND NORTHERN IRELAND
AND
THE GOVERNMENT OF THE PEOPLE'S REPUBLIC OF
CHINA
ON THE QUESTION OF HONG KONG

The Government of the United Kingdom of Great Britain and Northern Ireland and the Government of the People's Republic of China have reviewed with satisfaction the friendly relations existing between the two Governments and peoples in recent years and agreed that a proper negotiated settlement of the question of Hong Kong, which is left over from the past, is conducive to the maintenance of the prosperity and stability of Hong Kong and to the further strengthening and development of the relations between the two countries on a new basis. To this end, they have, after talks between the delegations of the two Governments, agreed to declare as follows:

1. The Government of the People's Republic of China declares that to recover the Hong Kong area (including Hong Kong Island, Kowloon and the New Territories, hereinafter referred to as Hong Kong) is the common aspiration of the entire Chinese people, and that it has decided to resume the exercise of sovereignty over Hong Kong with effect from 1 July 1997.

2. The Government of the United Kingdom declares that it will restore Hong Kong to the People's Republic of China with effect from 1 July 1997.

3. The Government of the People's Republic of China declares that the basic policies of the People's Republic of China regarding Hong Kong are as follows:

(1) Upholding national unity and territorial integrity and taking account of the history of Hong Kong and its realities, the People's Republic of China has decided to establish, in accordance with the provisions of Article 31 of the Constitution of the People's Republic of China, a Hong Kong Special Administrative Region upon resuming the exercise of sovereignty over Hong Kong.

(2) The Hong Kong Special Administrative Region will be directly under the authority of the Central People's Government of the People's Republic of China. The Hong Kong Special Administrative Region will enjoy a high degree of autonomy, except in foreign and defence affairs which are the responsibilities of the Central People's Government.

(3) The Hong Kong Special Administrative Region will be vested with executive, legislative and independent judicial power, including that of final adjudication. The laws currently in force in Hong Kong will remain basically unchanged.

(4) The Government of the Hong Kong Special Administrative Region will be composed of local inhabitants. The chief executive will be appointed by the Central People's Government on the basis of the results of elections or consultations to be held locally. Principal officials will be nominated by the chief executive of the Hong Kong Special Administrative Region for appointment by the Central People's Government. Chinese and foreign nationals

previously working in the public and police services in the government departments of Hong Kong may remain in employment. British and other foreign nationals may also be employed to serve as advisers or hold certain public posts in government departments of the Hong Kong Special Administrative Region.

(5) The current social and economic systems in Hong Kong will remain unchanged, and so will the life-style. Rights and freedoms, including those of the person, of speech, of the press, of assembly, of association, of travel, of movement, of correspondence, of strike, of choice of occupation, of academic research and of religious belief will be ensured by law in the Hong Kong Special Administrative Region. Private property, ownership of enterprises, legitimate right of inheritance and foreign investment will be protected by law.

(6) The Hong Kong Special Administrative Region will retain the status of a free port and a separate customs territory.

(7) The Hong Kong Special Administrative Region will retain the status of an international financial centre, and its markets for foreign exchange, gold, securities and futures will continue. There will be free flow of capital. The Hong Kong dollar will continue to circulate and remain freely convertible.

(8) The Hong Kong Special Administrative Region will have independent finances. The Central People's Government will not levy taxes on the Hong Kong Special Administrative Region.

(9) The Hong Kong Special Administrative Region may establish mutually beneficial economic relations with the United Kingdom and other countries, whose economic interests in Hong Kong will be given due regard.

(10) Using the name of "Hong Kong, China," the Hong Kong Special Administrative Region may on its own maintain and develop economic and cultural relations and conclude relevant agreements with states, regions and relevant international organisations.

The Government of the Hong Kong Special Administrative Region may on its own issue travel documents for entry into and exit from Hong Kong.

(11) The maintenance of public order in the Hong Kong Special Administrative Region will be the responsibility of the Government of the Hong Kong Special Administrative Region.

(12) The above-stated basic policies of the People's Republic of China regarding Hong Kong and the elaboration of them in Annex I to this Joint Declaration will be stipulated, in a Basic Law of the Hong Kong Special Administrative Region of the People's Republic of China, by the National People's Congress of the People's Republic of China, and they will remain unchanged for 50 years.

4. The Government of the United Kingdom and the Government of the People's Republic of China declare that, during the transitional period between the date of the entry into force of this Joint Declaration and 30 June 1997, the Government of the United Kingdom will be responsible for the administration of Hong Kong with the object of maintaining and preserving its economic prosperity and social stability; and that the Government of the People's Republic of China will give its cooperation in this connection.

5. The Government of the United Kingdom and the Government of the People's Republic of China declare that, in order to ensure a smooth transfer of government in

1997, and with a view to the effective implementation of this Joint Declaration, a Sino-British Joint Liaison Group will be set up when this Joint Declaration enters into force; and that it will be established and will function in accordance with the provisions of Annex II to this Joint Declaration.

6. The Government of the United Kingdom and the Government of the People's Republic of China declare that land leases in Hong Kong and other related matters will be dealt with in accordance with the provisions of Annex III to this Joint Declaration.

7. The Government of the United Kingdom and the Government of the People's Republic of China agree to implement the preceding declarations and the Annexes to this Joint Declaration.

8. This Joint Declaration is subject to ratification and shall enter into force on the date of the exchange of instruments of ratification, which shall take place in Beijing before 30 June 1985. This Joint Declaration and its Annexes shall be equally binding.

Done in duplicate at Beijing on   1984 in the English and Chinese languages, both texts being equally authentic.

For the
Government of the United Kingdom
of Great Britain and Northern Ireland

For the
Government of the
People's Republic of China

ANNEX I

ELABORATION BY THE GOVERNMENT OF THE PEOPLE'S REPUBLIC OF CHINA OF ITS BASIC POLICIES REGARDING HONG KONG

The Government of the People's Republic of China elaborates the basic policies of the People's Republic of China regarding Hong Kong as set out in paragraph 3 of the Joint Declaration of the Government of the United Kingdom of Great Britain and Northern Ireland and the Government of the People's Republic of China on the Question of Hong Kong as follows:

I

The Constitution of the People's Republic of China stipulates in Article 31 that "the state may establish special administrative regions when necessary. The systems to be instituted in special administrative regions shall be prescribed by laws enacted by the National People's Congress in the light of the specific conditions." In accordance with this Article, the People's Republic of China shall, upon the resumption of the exercise of sovereignty over Hong Kong on 1 July 1997, establish the Hong Kong Special Administrative Region of the People's Republic of China. The National People's Congress of the People's Republic of China shall enact and promulgate a Basic Law of the Hong Kong Special Administrative Region of the People's Republic of China (hereinafter referred to as the Basic Law) in accordance with the Constitution of the People's Republic of China, stipulating that after the establishment of the Hong Kong Special Administrative Region the socialist system and socialist policies shall not be practised in the Hong Kong Special Administrative Region and that Hong Kong's previous capitalist system and life-style shall remain unchanged for 50 years.

The Hong Kong Special Administrative Region shall be directly under the authority of the Central People's Government of the People's Republic of China and shall enjoy a high degree of autonomy. Except for foreign and defence affairs which are the responsibilities of the Central People's Government, the Hong Kong Special Administrative Region shall be vested with executive, legislative and independent judicial power, including that of final adjudication. The Central People's Government shall authorise the Hong Kong Special Administrative Region to conduct on its own those external affairs specified in Section XI of this Annex.

The government and legislature of the Hong Kong Special Administrative Region shall be composed of local inhabitants. The chief executive of the Hong Kong Special Administrative Region shall be selected by election or through consultations held locally and be appointed by the Central People's Government. Principal officials (equivalent to Secretaries) shall be nominated by the chief executive of the Hong Kong Special Administrative Region and appointed by the Central People's Government. The legislature of the Hong Kong Special Administrative Region shall be constituted by elections. The executive authorities shall abide by the law and shall be accountable to the legislature.

In addition to Chinese, English may also be used in organs of government and in the courts in the Hong Kong Special Administrative Region.

Apart from displaying the national flag and national emblem of the People's Republic of China, the Hong Kong Special Administrative Region may use a regional flag and emblem of its own.

II

After the establishment of the Hong Kong Special Administrative Region, the laws previously in force in Hong Kong (i.e. the common law, rules of equity, ordinances, subordinate legislation and customary law) shall be maintained, save for any that contravene the Basic Law and subject to any amendment by the Hong Kong Special Administrative Region legislature.

The legislative power of the Hong Kong Special Administrative Region shall be vested in the legislature of the Hong Kong Special Administrative Region. The legislature may on its own authority enact laws in accordance with the provisions of the Basic Law and legal procedures, and report them to the Standing Committee of the National People's Congress for the record. Laws enacted by the legislature which are in accordance with the Basic Law and legal procedures shall be regarded as valid.

The laws of the Hong Kong Special Administrative Region shall be the Basic Law, and the laws previously in force in Hong Kong and laws enacted by the Hong Kong Special Administrative Region legislature as above.

III

After the establishment of the Hong Kong Special Administrative Region, the judicial system previously practised in Hong Kong shall be maintained except for those changes consequent upon the vesting in the courts of the Hong Kong Special Administrative Region of the power of final adjudication.

Judicial power in the Hong Kong Special Administrative Region shall be vested in the courts of the Hong Kong Special Administrative Region. The courts shall exercise judicial power independently and free from any interference. Members of the judiciary shall be immune from legal action in respect of their judicial functions. The courts shall decide cases in accordance with the laws of the Hong Kong Special Administrative Region and may refer to precedents in other common law jurisdictions.

Judges of the Hong Kong Special Administrative Region courts shall be appointed by the chief executive of the Hong Kong Special Administrative Region acting in accordance with the recommendation of an independent commission composed of local judges, persons from the legal profession and other eminent persons. Judges shall be chosen by reference to their judicial qualities and may be recruited from other common law jurisdictions. A judge may only be removed for inability to discharge the functions of his office, or for misbehaviour, by the chief executive of the Hong Kong Special Administrative Region acting in accordance with the recommendation of a tribunal appointed by the chief judge of the court of final appeal, consisting of not fewer than three local judges. Additionally, the appointment or removal of principal judges (i.e. those of the highest rank) shall be made by the chief executive with the endorsement of the Hong Kong Special Administrative Region legislature and reported to the Standing Committee of the National People's Congress for the record. The system of appointment and removal of judicial officers other than judges shall be maintained.

The power of final judgment of the Hong Kong Special Administrative Region shall be vested in the court of final appeal in the Hong Kong Special Administrative Region, which may as required invite judges from other common law jurisdictions to sit on the court of final appeal.

A prosecuting authority of the Hong Kong Special Administrative Region shall control criminal prosecutions free from any interference.

On the basis of the system previously operating in Hong Kong, the Hong Kong Special Administrative Region Government shall on its own make provision for local lawyers and lawyers from outside the Hong Kong Special Administrative Region to work and practise in the Hong Kong Special Administrative Region.

The Central People's Government shall assist or authorise the Hong Kong Special Administrative Region Government to make appropriate arrangements for reciprocal juridical assistance with foreign states.

IV

After the establishment of the Hong Kong Special Administrative Region, public servants previously serving in Hong Kong in all government departments, including the police department, and members of the judiciary may all remain in employment and continue their service with pay, allowances, benefits and conditions of service no less favourable than before. The Hong Kong Special Administrative Region Government shall pay to such persons who retire or complete their contracts, as well as to those who have retired before 1 July 1997, or to their dependants, all pensions, gratuities, allowances and benefits due to them on terms no less favourable than before, and irrespective of their nationality or place of residence.

The Hong Kong Special Administrative Region Government may employ British and other foreign nationals previously serving in the public service in Hong Kong, and may recruit British and other foreign nationals holding permanent identity cards of the Hong Kong Special Administrative Region to serve as public servants at all levels, except as heads of major government departments (corresponding to branches or departments at Secretary level) including the police department, and as deputy heads of some of those departments. The Hong Kong Special Administrative Region Government may also employ British and other foreign nationals as advisers to government departments and, when there is a need, may recruit qualified candidates from outside the Hong Kong Special Administrative Region to professional and technical posts in government departments. The above shall be employed only in their individual capacities and, like other public servants, shall be responsible to the Hong Kong Special Administrative Region Government.

The appointment and promotion of public servants shall be on the basis of qualifications, experience and ability. Hong Kong's previous system of recruitment, employment, assessment, discipline, training and management for the public service (including special bodies for appointment, pay and conditions of service) shall, save for any provisions providing privileged treatment for foreign nationals, be maintained.

V

The Hong Kong Special Administrative Region shall deal on its own with financial matters, including disposing of its financial resources and drawing up its budgets and its final accounts. The Hong Kong Special Administrative Region shall report its budgets and final accounts to the Central People's Government for the record.

The Central People's Government shall not levy taxes on the Hong Kong Special Administrative Region. The Hong Kong Special Administrative Region shall use its financial revenues exclusively for its own purposes and they shall not be handed over to the Central People's Government. The systems by which taxation and public expenditure must be approved by the legislature, and by which there is accountability to the legislature for all public expenditure, and the system for auditing public accounts shall be maintained.

VI

The Hong Kong Special Administrative Region shall maintain the capitalist economic and trade systems previously practised in Hong Kong. The Hong Kong Special Administrative Region Government shall decide its economic and trade policies on its own. Rights concerning the ownership of property, including those relating to acquisition, use, disposal, inheritance and compensation for lawful deprivation (corresponding to the real value of the property concerned, freely convertible and paid without undue delay) shall continue to be protected by law.

The Hong Kong Special Administrative Region shall retain the status of a free port and continue a free trade policy, including the free movement of goods and capital. The Hong Kong Special Administrative Region may on its own maintain and develop economic and trade relations with all states and regions.

The Hong Kong Special Administrative Region shall be a separate customs territory. It may participate in relevant international organisations and international trade agreements (including preferential trade arrangements), such as the General Agreement on Tariffs and Trade and arrangements regarding international trade in textiles. Export quotas, tariff preferences and other similar arrangements obtained by the Hong Kong Special Administrative Region shall be enjoyed exclusively by the Hong Kong Special Administrative Region. The Hong Kong Special Administrative

Region shall have authority to issue its own certificates of origin for products manufactured locally, in accordance with prevailing rules of origin.

The Hong Kong Special Administrative Region may, as necessary, establish official and semi-official economic and trade missions in foreign countries, reporting the establishment of such missions to the Central People's Government for the record.

VII

The Hong Kong Special Administrative Region shall retain the status of an international financial centre. The monetary and financial systems previously practised in Hong Kong, including the systems of regulation and supervision of deposit-taking institutions and financial markets, shall be maintained.

The Hong Kong Special Administrative Region Government may decide its monetary and financial policies on its own. It shall safeguard the free operation of financial business and the free flow of capital within, into and out of the Hong Kong Special Administrative Region. No exchange control policy shall be applied in the Hong Kong Special Administrative Region. Markets for foreign exchange, gold, securities and futures shall continue.

The Hong Kong dollar, as the local legal tender, shall continue to circulate and remain freely convertible. The authority to issue Hong Kong currency shall be vested in the Hong Kong Special Administrative Region Government. The Hong Kong Special Administrative Region Government may authorise designated banks to issue or continue to issue Hong Kong currency under statutory authority, after satisfying itself that any issue of currency will be soundly based and that the arrangements for such issue are consistent with the object of maintaining the stability of the currency. Hong Kong currency bearing references inappropriate to the status of Hong Kong as a Special Administrative Region of the People's Republic of China shall be progressively replaced and withdrawn from circulation.

The Exchange Fund shall be managed and controlled by the Hong Kong Special Administrative Region Government, primarily for regulating the exchange value of the Hong Kong dollar.

VIII

The Hong Kong Special Administrative Region shall maintain Hong Kong's previous systems of shipping management and shipping regulation, including the system for regulating conditions of seamen. The specific functions and responsibilities of the Hong Kong Special Administrative Region Government in the field of shipping shall be defined by the Hong Kong Special Administrative Region Government on its own. Private shipping businesses and shipping-related businesses and private container terminals in Hong Kong may continue to operate freely.

The Hong Kong Special Administrative Region shall be authorised by the Central People's Government to continue to maintain a shipping register and issue related certificates under its own legislation in the name of "Hong Kong, China."

With the exception of foreign warships, access for which requires the permission of the Central People's Government, ships shall enjoy access to the ports of the Hong Kong Special Administrative Region in accordance with the laws of the Hong Kong Special Administrative Region.

IX

The Hong Kong Special Administrative Region shall maintain the status of Hong Kong as a centre of international and regional aviation. Airlines incorporated and having their principal place of business in Hong Kong and civil aviation related businesses may continue to operate. The Hong Kong Special Administrative Region shall continue the previous system of civil aviation management in Hong Kong, and keep its own aircraft register in accordance with provisions laid down by the Central People's Government concerning nationality marks and registration marks of aircraft. The Hong Kong Special Administrative Region shall be responsible on its own for matters of routine business and technical management of civil aviation, including the management of airports, the provision of air traffic services within the flight information region of the Hong Kong Special Administrative Region, and the discharge of other responsibilities allocated under the regional air navigation procedures of the International Civil Aviation Organisation.

The Central People's Government shall, in consultation with the Hong Kong Special Administrative Region Government, make arrangements providing for air services between the Hong Kong Special Administrative Region and other parts of the People's Republic of China for airlines incorporated and having their principal place of business in the Hong Kong Special Administrative Region and other airlines of the People's Republic of China. All Air Service Agreements providing for air services between other parts of the People's Republic of China and other states and regions with stops at the Hong Kong Special Administrative Region and air services between the Hong Kong Special Administrative Region and other states and regions with stops at other parts of the People's Republic of China shall be concluded by the Central People's Government. For this purpose, the Central People's Government shall take account of the special conditions and economic interests of the Hong Kong Special Administrative Region and consult the Hong Kong Special Administrative Region Government. Representatives of the Hong Kong Special Administrative Region Government may participate as members of delegations of the Government of the People's Republic of China in air service consultations with foreign governments concerning arrangements for such services.

Acting upon specific authorisations from the Central People's Government, the Hong Kong Special Administrative Region Government may:

— renew or amend Air Service Agreements and arrangements previously in force; in principle, all such Agreements and arrangements may be renewed or amended with the rights contained in such previous Agreements and arrangements being as far as possible maintained;

— negotiate and conclude new Air Service Agreements providing routes for airlines incorporated and having their principal place of business in the Hong Kong Special Administrative Region and rights for overflights and technical stops; and

— negotiate and conclude provisional arrangements where no Air Service Agreement with a foreign state or other region is in force.

All scheduled air services to, from or through the Hong Kong Special Administrative Region which do not operate to, from or through the mainland of China shall be regulated by Air Service Agreements or provisional arrangements referred to in this paragraph.

The Central People's Government shall give the Hong Kong Special Administrative Region Government the authority to:

— negotiate and conclude with other authorities all arrangements concerning the implementation of the above Air Service Agreements and provisional arrangements;

— issue licences to airlines incorporated and having their principal place of business in the Hong Kong Special Administrative Region;

— designate such airlines under the above Air Service Agreements and provisional arrangements; and

— issue permits to foreign airlines for services other than those to, from or through the mainland of China.

X

The Hong Kong Special Administrative Region shall maintain the educational system previously practised in Hong Kong. The Hong Kong Special Administrative Region Government shall on its own decide policies in the fields of culture, education, science and technology, including policies regarding the educational system and its administration, the language of instruction, the allocation of funds, the examination system, the system of academic awards and the recognition of educational and technological qualifications. Institutions of all kinds, including those run by religious and community organisations, may retain their autonomy. They may continue to recruit staff and use teaching materials from outside the Hong Kong Special Administrative Region. Students shall enjoy freedom of choice of education and freedom to pursue their education outside the Hong Kong Special Administrative Region.

XI

Subject to the principle that foreign affairs are the responsibility of the Central People's Government, representatives of the Hong Kong Special Administrative Region Government may participate, as members of delegations of the Government of the People's Republic of China, in negotiations at the diplomatic level directly affecting the Hong Kong Special Administrative Region conducted by the Central People's Government. The Hong Kong Special Administrative Region may on its own, using the name "Hong Kong, China," maintain and develop relations and conclude and implement agreements with states, regions and relevant international organisations in the appropriate fields, including the economic, trade, financial and monetary, shipping, communications, touristic, cultural and sporting fields. Representatives of the Hong Kong Special Administrative Region Government may participate, as members of delegations of the Government of the People's Republic of China, in international organisations or conferences in appropriate fields limited to states and affecting the Hong Kong Special Administrative Region, or may attend in such other capacity as may be permitted by the Central People's Government and the organisation or conference concerned, and may express their views in the name of "Hong Kong, China." The Hong Kong Special Administrative Region may, using the name "Hong Kong, China," participate in international organisations and conferences not limited to states.

The application to the Hong Kong Special Administrative Region of international agreements to which the People's Republic of China is or becomes a party shall be decided by the Central People's Government, in accordance with the circumstances and needs of the Hong Kong Special Administrative Region, and after seeking the views of the Hong Kong Special Administrative Region Government. International agreements to which the People's Republic of China is not a party but which are implemented in Hong Kong may remain implemented in the Hong Kong Special Administrative Region. The Central People's Government shall, as necessary, authorise or assist the Hong Kong Special Administrative Region Government to make appropriate arrangements for the application to the Hong Kong Special Administrative Region of other relevant international agreements. The Central People's Government shall take the necessary steps to ensure that the Hong Kong Special Administrative Region shall continue to retain its status in an appropriate capacity in those international organisations of which the People's Republic of China is a member and in which Hong Kong participates in one capacity or another. The Central People's Government shall, where necessary, facilitate the continued participation of the Hong Kong Special Administrative Region in an appropriate capacity in those international organisations in which Hong Kong is a participant in one capacity or another, but of which the People's Republic of China is not a member.

Foreign consular and other official or semi-official missions may be established in the Hong Kong Special Administrative Region with the approval of the Central People's Government. Consular and other official missions established in Hong Kong by states which have established formal diplomatic relations with the People's Republic of China may be maintained. According to the circumstances of each case, consular and other official missions of states having no formal diplomatic relations with the People's Republic of China may either be maintained or changed to semi-official missions. States not recognised by the People's Republic of China can only establish non-governmental institutions.

The United Kingdom may establish a Consulate-General in the Hong Kong Special Administrative Region.

XII

The maintenance of public order in the Hong Kong Special Administrative Region shall be the responsibility of the Hong Kong Special Administrative Region Government. Military forces sent by the Central People's Government to be stationed in the Hong Kong Special Administrative Region for the purpose of defence shall not interfere in the internal affairs of the Hong Kong Special Administrative Region. Expenditure for these military forces shall be borne by the Central People's Government.

XIII

The Hong Kong Special Administrative Region Government shall protect the rights and freedoms of inhabitants and other persons in the Hong Kong Special Administrative Region according to law. The Hong Kong Special Administrative Region Government shall maintain the rights and freedoms as provided for by the laws previously in force in Hong Kong, including freedom of the person, of speech, of the press, of assembly, of association, to form and join trade unions, of correspondence, of travel, of movement, of strike, of demonstration, of choice of occupation, of academic research, of belief, inviolability of the home, the freedom to marry and the right to raise a family freely.

Every person shall have the right to confidential legal advice, access to the courts, representation in the courts by lawyers of his choice, and to obtain judicial remedies. Every person shall have the right to challenge the actions of the executive in the courts.

Religious organisations and believers may maintain their relations with religious organisations and believers elsewhere, and schools, hospitals and welfare institutions run by religious organisations may be continued. The relationship between religious organisations in the Hong Kong Special Administrative Region and those in other parts of the People's Republic of China shall be based on the principles of non-subordination, non-interference and mutual respect.

The provisions of the International Covenant on Civil and Political Rights and the International Covenant on Economic, Social and Cultural Rights as applied to Hong Kong shall remain in force.

XIV

The following categories of persons shall have the right of abode in the Hong Kong Special Administrative Region, and, in accordance with the law of the Hong Kong Special Administrative Region, be qualified to obtain permanent identity cards issued by the Hong Kong Special Administrative Region Government, which state their right of abode:

— all Chinese nationals who were born or who have ordinarily resided in Hong Kong before or after the establishment of the Hong Kong Special Administrative Region for a continuous period of 7 years or more, and persons of Chinese nationality born outside Hong Kong of such Chinese nationals;

— all other persons who have ordinarily resided in Hong Kong before or after the establishment of the Hong Kong Special Administrative Region for a continuous period of 7 years or more and who have taken Hong Kong as their place of permanent residence before or after the establishment of the Hong Kong Special Administrative Region, and persons under 21 years of age who were born of such persons in Hong Kong before or after the establishment of the Hong Kong Special Administrative Region;

— any other persons who had the right of abode only in Hong Kong before the establishment of the Hong Kong Special Administrative Region.

The Central People's Government shall authorise the Hong Kong Special Administrative Region Government to issue, in accordance with the law, passports of the Hong Kong Special Administrative Region of the People's Republic of China to all Chinese nationals who hold permanent identity cards of the Hong Kong Special Administrative Region, and travel documents of the Hong Kong Special Administrative Region of the People's Republic of China to all other persons lawfully residing in the Hong Kong Special Administrative Region. The above passports and documents shall be valid for all states and regions and shall record the holder's right to return to the Hong Kong Special Administrative Region.

For the purpose of travelling to and from the Hong Kong Special Administrative Region, residents of the Hong Kong Special Administrative Region may use travel documents issued by the Hong Kong Special Administrative Region Government, or by other competent authorities of the People's Republic of China, or of other states. Holders of permanent identity cards of the Hong Kong Special Administrative Region may have this fact stated in their travel documents as evidence that the holders have the right of abode in the Hong Kong Special Administrative Region.

Entry into the Hong Kong Special Administrative Region of persons from other parts of China shall continue to be regulated in accordance with the present practice.

The Hong Kong Special Administrative Region Government may apply immigration controls on entry, stay in and departure from the Hong Kong Special Administrative Region by persons from foreign states and regions.

Unless restrained by law, holders of valid travel documents shall be free to leave the Hong Kong Special Administrative Region without special authorisation.

The Central People's Government shall assist or authorise the Hong Kong Special Administrative Region Government to conclude visa abolition agreements with states or regions.

ANNEX II

SINO-BRITISH JOINT LIAISON GROUP

1. In furtherance of their common aim and in order to ensure a smooth transfer of government in 1997, the Government of the United Kingdom and the Government of the People's Republic of China have agreed to continue their discussions in a friendly spirit and to develop the cooperative relationship which already exists between the two Governments over Hong Kong with a view to the effective implementation of the Joint Declaration.

2. In order to meet the requirements for liaison, consultation and the exchange of information, the two Governments have agreed to set up a Joint Liaison Group.

3. The functions of the Joint Liaison Group shall be:

(*a*) to conduct consultations on the implementation of the Joint Declaration;

(*b*) to discuss matters relating to the smooth transfer of government in 1997;

(*c*) to exchange information and conduct consultations on such subjects as may be agreed by the two sides.

Matters on which there is disagreement in the Joint Liaison Group shall be referred to the two Governments for solution through consultations.

4. Matters for consideration during the first half of the period between the establishment of the Joint Liaison Group and 1 July 1997 shall include:

(*a*) action to be taken by the two Governments to enable the Hong Kong Special Administrative Region to maintain its economic relations as a separate customs territory, and in particular to ensure the maintenance of Hong Kong's participation in the General Agreement on Tariffs and Trade, the Multifibre Arrangement and other international arrangements; and

(*b*) action to be taken by the two Governments to ensure the continued application of international rights and obligations affecting Hong Kong.

5. The two Governments have agreed that in the second half of the period between the establishment of the Joint Liaison Group and 1 July 1997 there will be need for closer cooperation, which will therefore be intensified during that period. Matters for consideration during this second period shall include:

(*a*) procedures to be adopted for the smooth transition in 1997;

(*b*) action to assist the Hong Kong Special Administrative Region to maintain and develop economic and cultural relations and conclude agreements on these matters with states, regions and relevant international organisations.

6. The Joint Liaison Group shall be an organ for liaison and not an organ of power. It shall play no part in the administration of Hong Kong or the Hong Kong Special

Administrative Region. Nor shall it have any supervisory role over that administration. The members and supporting staff of the Joint Liaison Group shall only conduct activities within the scope of the functions of the Joint Liaison Group.

7. Each side shall designate a senior representative, who shall be of Ambassadorial rank, and four other members of the group. Each side may send up to 20 supporting staff.

8. The Joint Liaison Group shall be established on the entry into force of the Joint Declaration. From 1 July 1988 the Joint Liaison Group shall have its principal base in Hong Kong. The Joint Liaison Group shall continue its work until 1 January 2000.

9. The Joint Liaison Group shall meet in Beijing, London and Hong Kong. It shall meet at least once in each of the three locations in each year. The venue for each meeting shall be agreed between the two sides.

10. Members of the Joint Liaison Group shall enjoy diplomatic privileges and immunities as appropriate when in the three locations. Proceedings of the Joint Liaison Group shall remain confidential unless otherwise agreed between the two sides.

11. The Joint Liaison Group may by agreement between the two sides decide to set up specialist sub-groups to deal with particular subjects requiring expert assistance.

12. Meetings of the Joint Liaison Group and sub-groups may be attended by experts other than the members of the Joint Liaison Group. Each side shall determine the composition of its delegation to particular meetings of the Joint Liaison Group or sub-group in accordance with the subjects to be discussed and the venue chosen.

13. The working procedures of the Joint Liaison Group shall be discussed and decided upon by the two sides within the guidelines laid down in this Annex.

ANNEX III

LAND LEASES

The Government of the United Kingdom and the Government of the People's Republic of China have agreed that, with effect from the entry into force of the Joint Declaration, land leases in Hong Kong and other related matters shall be dealt with in accordance with the following provisions:

1. All leases of land granted or decided upon before the entry into force of the Joint Declaration and those granted thereafter in accordance with paragraph 2 or 3 of this Annex, and which extend beyond 30 June 1997, and all rights in relation to such leases shall continue to be recognised and protected under the law of the Hong Kong Special Administrative Region.

2. All leases of land granted by the British Hong Kong Government not containing a right of renewal that expire before 30 June 1997, except short term tenancies and leases for special purposes, may be extended if the lessee so wishes for a period expiring not later than 30 June 2047 without payment of an additional premium. An annual rent shall be charged from the date of extension equivalent to 3 per cent of the rateable value of the property at that date, adjusted in step with any changes in the rateable value thereafter. In the case of old schedule lots, village lots, small houses and similar rural holdings, where the property was on 30 June 1984 held by, or, in the case of small houses granted after that date, the property is granted to, a person descended through the male line from a person who was in 1898 a resident of an established village in

Hong Kong, the rent shall remain unchanged so long as the property is held by that person or by one of his lawful successors in the male line. Where leases of land not having a right of renewal expire after 30 June 1997, they shall be dealt with in accordance with the relevant land laws and policies of the Hong Kong Special Administrative Region.

3. From the entry into force of the Joint Declaration until 30 June 1997, new leases of land may be granted by the British Hong Kong Government for terms expiring not later than 30 June 2047. Such leases shall be granted at a premium and nominal rental until 30 June 1997, after which date they shall not require payment of an additional premium but an annual rent equivalent to 3 percent of the rateable value of the property at that date, adjusted in step with changes in the rateable value thereafter, shall be charged.

4. The total amount of new land to be granted under paragraph 3 of this Annex shall be limited to 50 hectares a year (excluding land to be granted to the Hong Kong Housing Authority for public rental housing) from the entry into force of the Joint Declaration until 30 June 1997.

5. Modifications of the conditions specified in leases granted by the British Hong Kong Government may continue to be granted before 1 July 1997 at a premium equivalent to the difference between the value of the land under the previous conditions and its value under the modified conditions.

6. From the entry into force of the Joint Declaration until 30 June 1997, premium income obtained by the British Hong Kong Government from land transactions shall, after deduction of the average cost of land production, be shared equally between the British Hong Kong Government and the future Hong Kong Special Administrative Region Government. All the income obtained by the British Hong Kong Government, including the amount of the above mentioned deduction, shall be put into the Capital Works Reserve Fund for the financing of land development and public works in Hong Kong. The Hong Kong Special Administrative Region Government's share of the premium income shall be deposited in banks incorporated in Hong Kong and shall not be drawn on except for the financing of land development and public works in Hong Kong in accordance with the provisions of paragraph 7(d) of this Annex.

7. A Land Commission shall be established in Hong Kong immediately upon the entry into force of the Joint Declaration. The Land Commission shall be composed of an equal number of officials designated respectively by the Government of the United Kingdom and the Government of the People's Republic of China together with necessary supporting staff. The officials of the two sides shall be responsible to their respective governments. The Land Commission shall be dissolved on 30 June 1997.

The terms of reference of the Land Commission shall be:

(a) to conduct consultations on the implementation of this Annex;

(b) to monitor observance of the limit specified in paragraph 4 of this Annex, the amount of land granted to the Hong Kong Housing Authority for public rental housing, and the division and use of premium income referred to in paragraph 6 of this Annex;

(c) to consider and decide on proposals from the British Hong Kong Government for increasing the limit referred to in paragraph 4 of this Annex;

(d) to examine proposals for drawing on the Hong Kong Special Administrative Region Government's share of premium income referred to in paragraph 6 of this Annex and to make recommendations to the Chinese side for decision.

Matters on which there is disagreement in the Land Commission shall be referred to the Government of the United Kingdom and the Government of the People's Republic of China for decision.

8. Specific details regarding the establishment of the Land Commission shall be finalised separately by the two sides through consultations.

EXCHANGE OF MEMORANDA

(A) UNITED KINGDOM MEMORANDUM

In connection with the Joint Declaration of the Government of the United Kingdom of Great Britain and Northern Ireland and the Government of the People's Republic of China on the question of Hong Kong to be signed this day, the Government of the United Kingdom declares that, subject to the completion of the necessary amendments to the relevant United Kingdom legislation:

(a) All persons who on 30 June 1997 are, by virtue of a connection with Hong Kong, British Dependent Territories citizens (BDTCs) under the law in force in the United Kingdom will cease to be BDTCs with effect from 1 July 1997, but will be eligible to retain an appropriate status which, without conferring the right of abode in the United Kingdom, will entitle them to continue to use passports issued by the Government of the United Kingdom. This status will be acquired by such persons only if they hold or are included in such a British passport issued before 1 July 1997, except that eligible persons born on or after 1 January 1997 but before 1 July 1997 may obtain or be included in such a passport up to 31 December 1997.

(b) No person will acquire BDTC status on or after 1 July 1997 by virtue of a connection with Hong Kong. No person born on or after 1 July 1997 will acquire the status referred to as being appropriate in sub-paragraph (a).

(c) United Kingdom consular officials in the Hong Kong Special Administrative Region and elsewhere may renew and replace passports of persons mentioned in sub-paragraph (a) and may also issue them to persons, born before 1 July 1997 of such persons, who had previously been included in the passport of their parent.

(d) Those who have obtained or been included in passports issued by the Government of the United Kingdom under sub-paragraphs (a) and (c) will be entitled to receive, upon request, British consular services and protection when in third countries.

Beijing,   1984.

(B) CHINESE MEMORANDUM

The Government of the People's Republic of China has received the memorandum from the Government of the United Kingdom of Great Britain and Northern Ireland dated   1984.

Under the Nationality Law of the People's Republic of China, all Hong Kong Chinese compatriots, whether they are holders of the "British Dependent Territories citizens' Passport" or not, are Chinese nationals.

Taking account of the historical background of Hong Kong and its realities, the competent authorities of the Government of the People's Republic of China will, with effect from 1 July 1997, permit Chinese nationals in Hong Kong who were previously called "British Dependent Territories citizens" to use travel documents issued by the Government of the United Kingdom for the purpose of travelling to other states and regions.

The above Chinese nationals will not be entitled to British consular protection in the Hong Kong Special Administrative Region and other parts of the People's Republic of China on account of their holding the above-mentioned British travel documents.

Beijing,   1984.